Ignite Your Intrepid Soul

A courageous home for your human heart

KATIE BENWAY

Intrepid Eleven, LLC
www.intrepideleven.com

Printed in the United States of America.

Editor: Heather Doyle Fraser
Proofreader: Bridie O'Shaughnessy
Designer: Danielle Baird
Author Photo Credit: Corey Garland

ISBN: 978-1-7348010-1-9

Table of Contents

This book is dedicated...

To my children, Jack and Gus:

Thank you for choosing to journey with me in this life-time. Thank you for choosing me and trusting me to be your mom. You inspire me and heal me, you ground me and comfort me, you bring joy, irreverence, and blessed purpose to my life. You have shown me how to love myself, just by being who you are.

Remember, my loves: you are whole, always. You have access to all you need to know, always. You have a divine birthright to take in love, light, guidance, and comfort at any moment, at any time. You are never alone. You are never lost. You are beautiful forces of life, cradled, held, and nourished by the Universe, by your Spirit Guides, by your Souls, by me.

I am honored to be with each of you on your journeys to become the most vibrant expressions of your Souls you can be. My love, my light, my wisdom, my openness, my humility, my curiosity, and my unending commitment to awakening are always available to you. I am always available to you. With all of me, I love you, unconditionally and without end.

To the magical women who came before me:

To those who did not have the opportunities I have, who could not make the choices I am able to make, who dimmed their lights and made themselves smaller to survive physically, emotionally, and spiritually: I honor you and I thank you. The sacrifices you made to stay safe and the burdens you bore in the name of generational womanly duty have not been forgotten.

I hope that I, along with this book, contribute to the ending of a cycle of smallness suffered by women who were and are meant to be sweeping, magical, vibrant forces of creation and healing. I hope that I, in all of my freedom and safety in this lifetime, honor the freedom and safety you did not have. I hope that in living in my truth and in my vibrant magic, I may offer your legacies a home.

Introduction

I remember the day—the moment—I, on a human level, agreed to do this work. It was around 5:30 in the morning, the sun hadn't yet come up, and I woke up for seemingly no reason at all. I remember a resignation around being awake and knew that I couldn't go back to sleep, even if I tried. I had a few pristinely quiet hours to be alone, thoughtful, reflective, and open, and so I grabbed the book I'd been immersed in at that time.

I've devoured books my whole life, almost insatiably. I love learning, the ah-ha moment, sentences that stop me in my tracks, a turn of phrase that turns my thinking upside down. I like to be challenged and confronted with things that force me to pause. Language and the conveyance of new ideas have always fed my Soul and ignited my inner fire, my life force, and essence. And, so, the book I reached for that morning was no different. In fact, it was probably one of the most potent pieces of reading I'd ever done up until that point in my life.

The content transfixed me and the energy created in and around me while reading propelled me, effortlessly, page after page. The book was *The Testimony of Light: An Extraordinary Message of Life After Death*, by Helen Greaves, and it was, line by line, activating me, my life path, and my Soul in a way I'd never experienced before. I felt like everything in my world suddenly made sense.

The book offers a stunningly loving and gentle glimpse into life after death, delivered via channeled messages received and transcribed by Helen Greaves from her dear friend and Anglican nun, Frances Banks. When Frances passed away, Helen received several visitations and many profound messages from her lifelong friend on the Other Side. The book resonated with me in a way that I, at the time, wasn't able to fully understand, though I knew it was changing me in a real-time, moment-to-moment way. That one morning was no exception.

That morning, in my quiet resignation to wakefulness, I happened upon one particular passage that, somehow, someway, touched something so deep within my Soul, it unlocked a fully available pathway between my human self and my higher purpose. I had a moment of awakening, and it came fast and furiously, with or without my consent. It descended and struck, and *I was awake*.

I was stunned when I began to sob. It was a kind of crying I'd never experienced. Silently, huge tears poured down my face and I heaved for air as if I'd awoken from some oxygen-deprived state. But most puzzling to me at the time was that the sobbing and the torrent of energy pouring from me came without emotion. I wasn't sad or happy; I wasn't fearful or elated; I wasn't confused, daunted, panicked, or relieved. With these enormous tears that wouldn't let up, there was no emotion.

It was as if the act of reading this passage in this profound book reached into my being and connected my human self with my Soul. For the first time, in this lifetime, I had been awakened—literally and figuratively—and I was alive. And my whole body, my entire being, was releasing the energy of knowing, energy it had been containing and keeping safe for me for years. I was home: home within myself, home with my Soul, home with my purpose. My body knew it before I consciously did and the unlocking of this knowledge released a tidal wave of energy.

Drenched in tears, stunned as I searched to name what I was feeling (to no avail), I said, out loud, spontaneously, *"Okay, I'll do it. I'll do it."* And while I didn't recognize what was happening to me, I did recognize this: Helen Greaves, the perhaps accidental, yet totally willing and loving medium, was modeling what I was meant to do in this lifetime. I knew (despite avoiding it and squashing it and not admitting it to myself for years and years) that I'd been reading a book about my Soul's path and what I was meant to undertake in this human lifetime. I knew and had finally allowed myself to understand—and accept—consciously, that I had no choice but to begin the rest of my life in service to and alignment with this path. I'd have to re-start, re-organize, re-plan, re-birth...there was no other choice to make.

But my guides and the divine powers weren't quite done with me. As I dried my face, I heard, very clearly, *"Katie, your job is to clear the gray space. The gray space is cluttered. Help clear the gray space here and there."* And as awestruck, semi-confused, and stunned as I'd been that morning, this message about the gray space presented none of that for me. That is, I was utterly and completely clear about my job, my mission, my role. I knew, somehow, precisely what that message meant.

Perhaps I knew it, without explanation, because I'd firmly connected with my Soul, and its knowing had become, instantly, my human knowing. Perhaps the receipt and understanding of this message was the first piece of evidence that I had come into great alignment with my Soul.

As humans, we have experienced era after era of trauma, wounding, violence, and fear, and we have been unconsciously and consciously passing this on, generation after generation. We have struggled to accept our personal power to make deep, profound and sacred change—change that we are entirely capable of, both on a human level and a Soul level. Therefore, we clutter the "gray space."

The gray space is home to a collection of Souls who have become confused about the source of their personal power, unsure of their worthiness, and unclear about how to heal and transcend their heavier, karmic experiences. The gray space is an existential place of stuck energy that wants to be repaired, awoken, enlivened, loved, forgiven, and reunited with wholeness. The gray space is a place of separateness; the Universe is a place of wholeness.

Meanwhile, here on Earth, we have masses of humans steeped in trauma and wounding, searching for ways to feel better and find relief. So many people are struggling to become conscious and step into their personal power. Impacted by deep generational and long-held patterns of trauma and wounding, these are the very humans who may end up joining the gray space when they cross over. They may leave the Earth plane with unresolved feelings of unworthiness, guilt, shame, and pain, feeling somehow separate because of their earthly experiences. These feelings can continue into their afterlife.

At that moment, receiving that directive about "clearing the gray space," I knew and agreed to be one of the guides and facilitators here on Earth serving this larger mission. At that moment, I knew that my raw, natural ability to see, feel, sense, hear, and understand those on the Other Side, alongside my innate psychic and intuitive skills, had deep meaning and purpose. I was being asked to use these skills and abilities to connect the Souls on the Other Side with the humans here, for the express purpose of contributing to the healing of all involved. There was a reason I was born the way I was, a reason that Helen Greaves felt so familiar to me, and it was time.

So, here I am, a more than a decade out from that tear-filled morning of awakening. I'm a very busy working medium, psychic, and certified life coach. Daily, I help clear the gray space. When those on the Other Side come to visit, I help them connect with their loved ones: I give voice to their apologies and mea culpas and I share their regrets, misgivings, insights, stories, explanations, and messages. I act as the go-between as their loved ones ask questions and search for meaning. And, as these Souls connect to and offer whatever is necessary for the human in front of me to heal, all involved are lifted and evolved.

As these Souls forgive themselves, heal, and reconnect with love, they evolve, rising out of the gray space and into the freedom of light and awareness. They become less separate and more merged with the wholeness of the Universe.

Meanwhile, often, the power of connecting with a loved one on the Other Side leaves the human sitting on my couch feeling lighter, brighter, less guilt-ridden or sad, and more aware that Souls live on. In this way, these connections help people become more conscious and less wounded. Awakened and healed people don't get caught up in the gray space.

When we, in human form or Soul form, make the conscious choice to heal, a robust, reverberating process begins. Not only do we lift and awaken ourselves, but also our children, our parents, our siblings, and our ancestors. The power of one awakened Soul, choosing to be in loving alignment, is potent and supremely divine. Every Soul in the Universe is touched when one Soul awakens.

I wrote this book to share what I've learned. I wrote this book to help clear the gray space.

As a student of the Universe, I have witnessed and observed the richness of the messages I have been asked to convey over the years. I am still the reader and witness, devouring new books, new insights, new concepts, new healing perspectives, as I encounter them. I am with you, journeying, one step at a time, learning to love myself, heal myself, and take continued responsibility for myself and what I put out into the Universe. I am walking my talk because, as I've learned, there is nothing more important than transcending the human experience and returning to the Soul.

How to Use This Book

This book is an invitation. It's an invitation to you to take what resonates, question or leave what doesn't, be inspired by something new, gain spiritual perspective, and be curious about yourself. This book isn't one-size-fits-all; it's a welcome to find your center, your Soul, your process, your voice, your place of insight, and your healing path. There is no pressure or judgment, and there is no timeline or rush. This is *your* process.

---♥---

We'll begin by grounding and discovering where your Soul Fire lives. You'll get to know that Soul Fire, what feeds it, what depletes it, how it speaks to you, and how you can communicate with it. You'll return, throughout this book and this journey, to your Soul Fire, through sacred intention-setting exercises. We are cultivating your Soul Fire and strengthening your relationship with it so that you may carry it, consciously, with you every day. Together, we'll build a strong foundation and understanding so that you can create practices, habits, and routines that support your relationship with your Soul.

——————————————— ♥ ———————————————

While writing this book, it became clear that I needed to include channeled messages from the Other Side. When I received these messages, the tone and tenor were specific, and there was very obviously a gravity and sacredness to the content. It was clear these messages were essential to include in the book because they are necessary for each reader. You'll find these messages throughout the book, entitled "A Message from the Other Side." I hope you find them as compelling and thought-provoking as I do. They were given to me for you.

——————————————— ♥ ———————————————

I am using the word "Universe" in this book because that is how I think about the constant, undying, powerful, loving force surrounding and cradling all of us. You are welcome to replace "Universe" with any word that works for you: Source, God, Creator, Spirit, All, etc.

——————————————— ♥ ———————————————

While this book offers a progression of ideas and concepts, you may choose to come back to components of this book over time. There is no need to read it all, or in order; take what you need, when you need it.

———————————— ♥ ————————————

When you're reading this book and something resonates, it's resonating with you: your Soul, your Soul Fire, your personal seat of power.

The experience of resonance comes in different forms for each of us. You might feel something physical, like a chill throughout your body or the feeling of something heavy hitting your gut. You might have a spontaneous emotional reaction, laughing, or ah-ha-ing, or suddenly bursting into tears. You might see a snapshot of an event in your life, remember someone from your family or earlier life, or experience an old memory. You may suddenly see a pattern, habit, or theme that's been pervasive in your life through a different lens or in a completely different way. You may recognize what's coming up for you, or you may not.

When this happens, please don't worry if you are not able to readily name or understand what's coming up. The value is simply acknowledging and honoring that something resonates with you, and that resonance has released or activated something within your Soul. In that resonating and releasing, a new insight, connection, or pathway is being offered to you. There is no need to understand what's being revealed or shifted immediately—this will often unfold over time, in its own time.

All you need to do when something resonates is notice, acknowledge, and honor it.

Take it in, write it down, highlight the page, or the sentence. Keep a notebook or journal nearby so that you can honor yourself and what resonates with you by writing it down. Or, pause, close the book, close your eyes, and feel the experience of deep, personal resonance. Imagine bringing what you've found back to your Soul Fire or allowing it to permeate your physical being.

Develop your own way of receiving resonant insights and your personal practice of noticing, acknowledging, and honoring them with openness, warmth, love, and gentle curiosity.

Moments of resonance are loving gifts from your Soul. In them, there is no pressure or demand, there is simply a loving revealing of truth that is now available to you. Truth doesn't expire, you can always return to it, again and again.

———————————— ♥ ————————————

Finally, I often remind my clients of this, and I will offer it to you, dear reader:

Yes, I am a psychic and a medium; yes, I am a trained life coach. But, what I do is not more powerful than you, your Soul, and your free will. That my Soul, in this lifetime, agreed to be a human with significant psychic access does not mean that my intuition outweighs your own. Yes, I agreed to take on some of these tools so that I may be a helpful teacher and guide, but you have your own tool kit, filled with tools precisely-crafted for you. Never forget your own power, truth, and wholeness.

My role is that of reminder. My purpose is to amplify intuition—your home-made, grown-in-the-soil-of-your-Soul inner voice. My part is to remind you of the perennial, never-ending existence of your Soul's intuitive voice and that your life offers constant reminders of the presence of that voice. My role is to remind you that you are the seat of your own power.

I won't tell you anything that you don't already know. You may not consciously be aware of something, or it might have previously shown up to you as a foggy, nagging thought, feeling, or idea, but there isn't anything that you need to know that you don't already know. You have intrinsic access to the answers and insights you need, to the truths that unlock and break through the confusion, and to the path to your Soul.

*"During life, keep death on your shoulder
and identify with your Soul."*

—Ram Dass

———————————— ♥ ————————————

*"We are travelers on a cosmic journey, stardust, swirling
and dancing in the eddies and whirlpools of infinity. Life
is eternal. We have stopped for a moment to encounter
each other, to meet, to love, to share. This is a precious
moment. It is a little parenthesis in eternity."*

—Paulo Coelho, *The Alchemist*

Part One

Returning to the Soul

"My soul is from elsewhere, I'm sure of that, and I intend to end up there."

—Rumi

♥

"The soul is the truth of who we are."

—Marianne Williamson

A Grounded Beginning

You are deeply, profoundly, magnificently powerful. You, in your human body, with your wandering mind, your emotional ebbs and flows, your questions and longings, have access to divine wisdom *all the time*. You are the seat of your power and are so much more than you've believed you are.

You are one decision, one ah-ha moment, one mindset shift, one emotional clearing, one intuitive insight away from taking the next right, authentic step on your journey. And because you are so powerful, so are your choices. What you choose either harnesses or stifles the power of your Soul.

You see, the premise of the Universe is that small, often seemingly insignificant acts offer substantial impact on the much larger system. The Universe, in all of its vastness and infiniteness, isn't requiring us to be big, sweeping giants of tsunami-sized change. No. It's inviting us to be just the way we are and to do what we're capable of doing. To be the size and scope that we are, here on Earth, and do what's squarely within our power, making choices and taking steps.

Why?

The answer is powerfully simple: *This whole system— the Universe—is designed to bring us to the realization that small acts propel the grand picture.* The divine order intends to bring us to the place where we become empowered and transformed by taking small steps and making single choices toward a broader vision or a deeper truth. The Universe is training us to realize that power lies within us, in every step we take, in each of our single small actions.

> *In a show of perpetual love and commitment to evolution, the Universe constantly creates opportunities for us to believe, sacredly, in ourselves and the power of intentioned, conscious choice.*

We are meant to come to understand that our perceived smallness, in relation to the untold expansiveness of the Universe, reveals to us our most profound truth: that we are the root of our power. We are meant to transcend our perceptions that we are powerless and come to know and experience how powerful we are.

This macro/micro relationship that often overwhelms the human mind is here to show us that there is nothing to do but begin with ourselves, at the individual level, with choice, intention, free will, goodness, love, faith, curiosity, and optimism. And, if you can't carry all of that, all of the time (and who can?), then at the very least, this beautiful divine bigness is asking us not to become lost in the misconception that we are small, insignificant, or powerless.

The invitation to take small, individual steps helps to illuminate the power we have to make conscious change, initiating brilliant ripple effects and altering our own lives for the better.

The divine system, on the whole, is purposely so grand that the only thing you can do is start with you, wherever you are, with what you know, with what you have, right now. The Universe wants to lead you back to your seat of inner wisdom and power, where you can come to know and heal yourself deeply, and then come into greater alignment with your Soul, one step at a time.

The Spiritual and Mystical Path of the Soul Is Always Available to You

Your Soul has always been there, all along, through it all. Its call to you has never gone away; your perception might have been that the call has been fainter or louder at times. You might have even felt that its call went silent or that it raged ferociously at you, through a tragic life event. Throughout it all, whatever your relationship to it, your Soul has always been with you, inviting you home.

Your Soul does not die. It does not judge, nor does it love conditionally. It is steadfast and constant. And, it has been asking you, through your life experiences, to return to it.

Your Soul invites you to look at life spiritually, through a mystical lens. Your Soul wants to help you find clarity and personal understanding through spiritual self-discovery. Your Soul does its best work when you remember that you're a spiritual being, and when you embark upon a spiritual journey.

> *And so, at any moment, just as you are, you can choose to seek your Soul, walk toward it, return to it, and align with it.*

Aligning with your Soul is a journey that doesn't discriminate. It doesn't prefer the wealthy or the seasoned; it doesn't cater to the spiritually "awake" or avid retreat-goers; it doesn't care about your mistakes or failings, your shame, or your guilt. It doesn't matter where you are on your life's journey; you can start from anywhere. You can, on any day, at any moment, decide that you're ready to begin to move toward your Soul and head off, along the pathway of self-love and self-discovery.

Your Soul is unconditionally inviting and will always receive you. *Always.*

The Power of Beginning

The reason that it doesn't much matter where we are or how we define ourselves or what terrible trouble we've gotten into is that we are beings who like beginnings. Beginnings speak to us, empower us, motivate us. They provide us with invaluable sparks of hope, optimism, vision, and faith. It's natural to begin, to trip up, and then start again. To die and then be reborn.

Our hard-wiring prompts us to seek our Souls, whether we know and accept this truth or not. And so, it doesn't much matter where you think or judge yourself to be, what matters is this: *In reading this book, your Soul is asking you to begin something. Whatever that is, you're ready for it. You wouldn't be reading this, right now, if you weren't.*

It doesn't matter where you are or where you've been or whether you've got a kind narrative you dictate to yourself or an abusive one. It doesn't matter if you have years of experience in doing your inner work, or going to therapy, or sitting high on a mountaintop in silent meditation. It doesn't matter if you don't know what it means to be spiritual or have no clue what it means to heal yourself.

You don't need to accomplish or resolve any of this before you start.

You see, the Universe is kind. Your Soul is kind. Your task is to consider being kind to yourself, and if that's too tall an order right now, then begin with acceptance and allowance. Accept yourself and all that brought you here; accept and allow that your Soul asks you to love and care for yourself with compassion; accept and allow that your pace is sacred and your own. There is no one judging or timing your progress, declaring winners and losers. *You are right where you're meant to be.*

Your Soul won't let you down. Your Soul will guide you and show you what you need to see, understand, and address. You are ready to love and support yourself. You are ready to align courageously with your Soul. You are ready to get to know your Soul like never before and build fearless intimacy with it. You are ready to make your human life more congruent with your Soul.

The Universe and your Soul have been conspiring to bring you to the place where you know the only thing you can do is take a single step, a single action, on the spiritual and mystical path within. All of this has been about you arriving at the place where you are ready to begin.

Finding, Cultivating, and Nourishing Your Soul Fire

Let's begin by centering your awareness and coming to the grounded beginning: the place where your Soul Fire lives.

Let's root and ground in this beautiful, forgiving, loving, and optimistic space of beginning. Let's build a place where your mindset shifts from one of hard work to one of gentle curiosity.

Here, you don't need to pursue something intensely; you simply need to open gently.

With gentle curiosity, open to the possibility of releasing what needs to be released, of allowing what needs to be allowed, and of expanding what needs to be expanded.

This place is steadfast, eternal, and powerful while offering grace, invitation, and gentleness.

This place contains the deep knowledge that one small choice, shift, or action has the power to transform your life.

Here, you know that these small, intentioned steps offer you access to the magnificent, loving, helpful energy provided by the Universe.

Here, you know that building alignment with your Soul comes with one intentioned step at a time. Here, you know that your power lies within you and within your choice to step forward.

In this place, we'll build and cultivate your Soul Fire. This Fire is yours, your birthright. This Fire is the spark of the Universe within you. This Fire offers a place of return, beginning, and alignment. This Fire offers you rest, comfort, and a grounded center. This Fire is where your Soul lives. This Fire is your home and the doorstep to your Highest Self.

This Fire is the essential expression of your Soul, and its flames offer you:

• Acceptance of your life, your current state, where you've been, your mistakes, your triumphs, and all that brought you to where you now are.

• Allowance of what has been, what is, and what is to come.

- Intentions of release, healing, and transformation.

- Self-compassion, self-trust, and self-love.

- Deepened relationships with curiosity, truth, and ease.

These are flames that never die; they are always here for you. They are yours. Always.

Breathe. See this Fire. Envision yourself sitting next to it.

Together, on this journey and throughout this book, we will return here, to this Fire. On your own, at any time, you can return to this Fire.

This place, this Soul Fire, is yours and you are always welcome here.

SACRED INTENTION-SETTING:
Welcoming the Soul Fire

Spend the time you need to read these words, breathing, quieting your body and your mind, and cultivating this vision or sense of your Soul Fire. This exercise is worth your time, so be *here*: envisioning, sensing, feeling, and experiencing for as long as feels right and complete. As you do, become open to setting an intention—a sacred dog-earring of this momentous page in the book of your journey.

When you're ready, read silently or aloud this intention:

I allow connection with my Soul. I allow the flames of my Soul Fire to direct and nurture me.

I allow myself to receive and to know that I am worthy.

I allow myself to receive the things that are in my Highest and Best Honor, even when I am unsure that I am worthy of them.

I allow curiosity about the next step on the journey toward my Soul.

I allow myself the time and space to honor, understand, heal, and consider the messages my Soul has for me.

I allow unconditional love.

POWERING INTENTION
WITH ACTION

Consider pairing this intention with an action step or two. Consider returning, on your own, to your Soul Fire, to inquire and sit, from time to time. How might you come to know, more closely, your Soul Fire? Consider revisiting this intention with curiosity about what you, in your conscious daily life, have been able to allow or what has been more difficult to allow. If there's anything that you felt resistance to allowing, see if you can soften that resistance and open up just a bit more. Consider taking a gentle, right step toward getting to know your Soul Fire and what a relationship with your Soul Fire would look like.

"We are not human beings having a spiritual experience.
We are spiritual beings having a human experience."

—Pierre Teilhard de Chardin

———————————————— ♥ ————————————————

"The act of discovering who we are will force us to
accept that we can go further than we think."

—Paulo Coelho

Chapter One

You Are a Soul

Your Soul is the constant; human bodies die and pass away, but Souls do not die or cease to exist. Like all energy within the Universe, Souls change shape and form, shift, and grow. Our human incarnations vary in length, circumstance, and theme, reflecting the evolutionary nature of our Souls. We have many lifetimes, designed to immerse us in experiences that, ideally and ultimately, prompt us to grow, heal, and evolve.

Your Soul carries the knowledge of what you intend to accomplish in your lifetime and is continually revealing to you that more substantial, higher path through life events and experiences. There isn't one predestined path for you within a lifetime; there are countless ways in which you can learn lessons and grow. There is, however, a singular, reliable, though sometimes subtle, current that carries you throughout your lifetime.

That current represents the overarching intentions of your Soul. Just as a current within a body of water might, it maintains its strength and purpose while allowing for other movements: free will, choice, breakdowns, awakenings—all the messiness, bumps, bruises, and triumphs of the human experience. That powerful invisible current always returns you, whether you're aware of it or not, or like it or not, to the lessons your Soul intends to learn, in your human lifetime.

Because you have this current keeping you on track (even when you fear you're woefully off track), you always have the opportunity to return to your Soul path. Every day, every moment, it's still there for you, always beckoning you to return to it, asking you to notice it and, ultimately, to give yourself over to it.

This beckoning is constant because of its higher and noble purpose: when each of us aligns with our Souls, our consciousness expands, perceptions shift, and significant evolution occurs. Aligning with the Soul is sacred and divine. When we align with our Souls and endeavor to build human lives that are congruent with our Souls, we become instantly more in touch with our own light and, therefore, put more light out into the Universe.

> *There is a momentous call for each of us to awaken, become more conscious, and align with our Souls. That call is coming from the Universe, across timeframes and dimensions, from divine forces far and wide.*

That call asks Souls on the Other Side and in the gray space to awaken and merge with the light, and it asks humans to take personal responsibility, step into their power, and heal. The call asks each of us to become aware and responsible and to align with our highest expression. It asks all of us to shed the illusion of our human experiences and become consciously united with our divine, light-filled nature, and to translate that union into personal power, choice, free will, and action.

This divine call to awaken asks each of us to love ourselves with new, fierce bravery, and to believe in the sacred and sweeping power of love to heal and unite. It asks us to treat ourselves with respect, kindness, compassion, and tender curiosity. The call asks us to take full responsibility for ourselves, our choices, thoughts, behaviors, actions, and energy.

> *Ultimately, this call asks us to remember and return to a deep, profound truth: we are Souls, exquisitely connected to a divine and unconditionally loving force. We are deeply worthy of this force and invited, daily, to embody it in our human lives.*

You have probably heard and felt this call. It feels urgent at times, doesn't it? It feels like we need to awaken and evolve. It feels like it's time for humanity to get ahold of itself and regain a sacred, spiritual center, doesn't it? If you've heard and recognized this call you're ready to return to your Soul.

A Message from the Other Side

"Align with your Soul, and you align with the Universe. Align with your Soul, and you align with divine essence, life force itself. There's magic, peace, and ease to harness there. There is clarity and understanding there. It's a beautiful place to visit, and you must return to it, time and time again, to make it your default. To ingrain the pathway so that there is no other. The

power of a single human aligned with their Soul is magnificent and beyond measure. How much change could occur, how much light could shine, if humans no longer doubted the existence of their Souls?"

Your Humanness Does Not Define You

Becoming human is how your Soul has chosen to incarnate in this lifetime—it's how your Soul has chosen to learn, grow, heal, and evolve. Your Soul is the truest thing about you, and your human experience is a powerful tool meant to teach you where and how to find your Soul.

The Soul is constant. The human experience, meanwhile, is fleeting. *The human experience does not define us; we are not meant to become what we experience as humans.* That's slippery territory, in fact: when we mistake our human experiences for definitive statements about who and what we are; or when we *become* what we experience rather than allow experience to change, refine, shift, and evolve us.

It's fitting to begin this chapter with a powerfully accurate insight about the nature of the Soul and the human experience from a French man. You see, the French language has something to teach us here. In the English language, we say, "I am hungry" or "I am tired" or "I am angry." While, in the French language, these phrases look more like this: "I have hunger" or "I have fatigue" or "I have anger." In the French language, it's clear that the human is *experiencing* these states of being, rather than *becoming* them. The French language makes clear that human experiences or emotional states are fleeting or passing. It's a profound distinction—one that leads us to an equally profound pivot point.

Understanding Your Relationship to the Human Experience

There is, for sure, a delicate balance here. We are meant to experience being human, all the highs and lows, tragedies, and triumphs, the moments that flatten us and those that enliven us. We are here to *do* this. That you're human is no accident; it's highly intentional, and your Soul wants you to be in this human experience. It's messy, and it's wild, and you're supposed to get dirty.

> *Your Soul does not want you to become your human experience or allow it to diminish or destroy you. Your Soul wants what you experience to inform you, to move through you, and ultimately, to change you. Your Soul wants you to keep the human experience active rather than letting it settle, dormant and definitive inside of you.*

Incarnating as a human being—living a human life—is a process of being activated and changed. It's an alchemical process whereby steady pressure is applied to create transformation.

And you can count on your human life to do just that—to apply steady pressure: steady pressure in the form of tragedy and suffering; in joy and connection; in abundance and lack; in new ideas and tricky problems. In the moments of disillusionment, fatigue, and confusion, when you feel rudderless and unsure of where you belong and where you should go, you will find the steady pressure of life. And in the moments of connection, understanding, clarity, and alignment where you feel totally alive and vibrant, you'll discover life's invitation to evolve—to reach for more. In hearing the right messages at the right times, reading books that blow your mind, encountering teachers that provide sacred moments of illumination, in relationships, good and bad, you'll be presented with just what you need to take your next, right step.

All of life is a steady application of pressure designed to bring you into deeper relationship and alignment with your Soul.

Whether we experience that pressure as positive or negative, this is the Universal force of transformation carried by our Souls. The human experience is an expression of the Universal force of transformation and change. It is constant and unyielding. Accept it, allow it, surrender to it, and work with it and you'll experience a knowing, belonging, and peace that only your Soul can provide. You'll experience the feeling of being on your path.

Allow your life to change you. Let it change your mind, let it educate you, let it expand you, let it build your empathy, let it show you how to love yourself, let it make you different from what you were.

Work with your life, knowing that what it presents to you, good or bad, amounts to a series of invitations to get to know your deepest self and to remember your Soul.

Your Human Experiences Are
Your Personal Compass

Our Souls want us to understand that our humanness is informative, acting as a compass, and providing insightful direction. If you can regard your human experience as offering clues to what you need to see, know, accept, understand, release, and heal, you'll experience what life wants to teach you, rather than feeling like life is exacting merciless control over you.

Ultimately, your human experiences are revealing what inside you needs your attention and healing, so that you can cultivate a deeper relationship with your Soul.

If you allow your life experiences to show you where you can grow, heal, and evolve, you'll build a life that is congruent with your Soul. You'll be working with the universal force of transformation.

Interestingly, it's often the most human of experiences, from losing a job or the breakup of a relationship to an illness or the death of a loved one, that bring us to this precipice of transformation. This is a place where, in our desire to find reason or relief, we discover an innate longing to align with our own Soul. Here, we begin asking deeper, more spiritual questions. We find our intrinsic desire for spiritual language and a spiritual way of bringing meaning to what we're experiencing. On our knees, in the depths of suffering or confusion, throwing our hands up and releasing it all, we find ourselves in a profound place of transformation. It's our human experiences that bring us right there.

Here, we're willing to give up whatever isn't working (and at these moments, most of us don't know precisely what isn't working, we just know something isn't) and instead are ready to accept a new way of viewing and relating to our lives and the world.

People often ask about the purpose of suffering. The truth is that pain is where we often find our most significant insights and moments of transformation. Suffering is the place that forces us to go inward because what's happening outside of us feels so hurtful, confusing, tragic, chaotic, or exhausting. Suffering propels us out of the human experience and into ourselves, toward our Souls, toward a spiritual path and paradigm. Suffering reminds us that the ultimate answer is to go inward, to return to the home our Souls provide.

And just when you thought the Universe and your Soul sounded punitive or fond of pain, there's the joy. And the contentment. And the beauty. There are feelings of lightness and wholeness when you're doing what nourishes your Soul: singing, playing music, writing, or reading; playing with children you love, delighting in the sound of their laughter; running a few miles or stretching into your favorite yoga pose; wrapped in the arms of your true love or engrossed in conversation with a best friend. Life teaches us in these moments, too.

These moments of joy, freedom, lightness, contentment, and connection serve to show us what is true. These moments of delight, being understood, and touching the meaning of life, teach us where our Souls live and remind us of our capacity as human beings to create more of these moments. We can seek out these moments and string them together, making them the rule rather than the exception.

The Universe's ability to balance all within it is reflected in the never-ending exercise of opposite, yet co-working forces: yin and yang, dark and light, death and rebirth. There is suffering, yes, just as there, too, is joy. There is separation and confusion, just as there is union and clarity.

Remember: the hard times teach us, grow us, evolve us, but so do the good times. You have the power to note those moments of beauty and fullness, and to say, right then and there, *"This! More of this! I choose THIS."*

In this way, the experiences we have as humans endeavor to remind us about ourselves: where we're blocked and free, where we need healing and more conscious awareness, or where we need added intention to multiply what's right and good. Whether identifying and duplicating moments of joy or acknowledging something needing healing, we are wired to seek order, to find a way to make sense of our existence. Our life experiences prompt us to give up old ways of being, to take leaps of faith, to decide to heal, change, expand, and honor ourselves in new and unconditionally loving ways. If we allow the experiences of life to penetrate us, move through us, and inform us, they'll spur us onto a spiritual path that inherently heals and makes sense of the human experience.

You came here to experience the essence of human life, and that's a truth that won't ever change, fade, or give up on you. You are here to come to know that, one way or another, the only place to go is in, and by going within, you will find your Soul.

A Message from the Other Side

"Your Soul longs for where you originated. There, existence is expansive, loving, infinite, and true. It's normal to feel constricted in the human incarnation on the Earth plane. You have a body, you feel the communal fears of your societies, you can only "see" as much as your awareness allows. Such is the human experience. You will feel smaller, constricted, and you will miss where you came from. Please accept this. The discomfort that comes from feeling this constriction will prompt your growth, fuel your quest for perspective, expand your awareness,

and provoke deep cellular memories of where you came from and the truths you carry. Please accept the longing; welcome the longing; follow the longing. It will lead you home to your Soul. It will lead you to create a home where you are, in the incarnation you're in, on the Earth plane. This is what you've intended to do."

Your Soul Comes Prepared

We can't understand the full scope of the Universe, not with our human faculties, and that's okay—because we've come here with powerful tools, carried within the Soul. All of these innate tools, including curiosity, resilience, persistence, a belief in more, and our intuition, help illuminate the pathway to greater understanding. These tools help us build self-trust, know and understand ourselves, and return us to a spiritual center when things get chaotic.

As humans, we are innately curious. We are wired to evolve, ask questions, wonder, adjust, and grow. We are wired for resilience and persistence—to keep trying. It's these Universal, yet very personal, forces, held within, that carry us to the place where the Soul does its best work: healing, restoring, rebirthing, releasing, leap-of-faith-ing, transforming. These forces propel us to that place where no suitable cognitive answer comes, and therefore we must jump or leap or try or change, often in a direction that feels new, less familiar, and scary.

You can trust what you've come here with and what resides within you, even if you have yet to identify it or you feel it needs strengthening or focus. You've come with what you need to engage in this human experience and allow it to transform you. You can trust your Soul, along with the forces of truth and tools of perseverance and clarity it carries.

 ## SACRED INTENTION-SETTING:
Understanding the Tools Your Soul Offers

We're going to deepen our understanding and exploration of the Soul and the tools it offers us throughout this book. For now, let's return to your Soul Fire to discover and further understand the personal tool kit your Soul carries for you. What forces, skills, talents, or qualities is your Soul carrying and offering to you to help guide and ease your journey?

When you're ready, read silently or aloud this intention:

Sitting next to my Soul Fire, I welcome its wisdom and insight. I appreciate and receive, with gratitude and joy, my Soul's tool kit. I note what this tool kit looks like, the container itself, and then, what this container carries.

I note the guiding forces, elements of my human personality, Universal forces, skills, and talents that are offered to me by my Soul as tools to help ground and power my personal life journey. I ask my Soul Fire to show me and teach me about each tool.

I accept that these tools are my birthright and here for me to use because I am worthy, loved, and valued. I accept the gift of this tool kit and pledge to explore and understand each of the tools it contains, for I know that each one offers divine assistance.

POWERING INTENTION WITH ACTION

Consider creating a drawing or writing a narrative about your Soul's tool kit. How does it look? How does it feel? Do you recognize it in any way? Then, draw or write about each of the tools contained within your Soul's tool kit. Consider these questions: What do each of these tools offer you? How do they feel? How do these tools show up in your daily life? Does one tool feel more comfortable to you than another? Does one call to you more prominently than another? Which tool should you work with at this time?

"The intuitive mind is a sacred gift, and the rational mind is the faithful servant. We have created a society that honors the servant and has forgotten the gift."

—Albert Einstein

♥

"Intuition is really a sudden immersion of the soul into the universal current of life."

—Paulo Coelho, *The Alchemist*

Chapter Two

Your Intuition Is
Your Soul's Voice

When our Souls incarnate into human bodies, we agree to the illusory nature of the human experience. Part of that illusion is that we are separate from the Universe. Some spiritual and mystical teachers even go as far as to say that a prerequisite of the incarnation gig is that we forget where we come from, we forget that we are Souls, and that the human journey is one of remembering.

Whether that forgetting is the price of admission or merely a by-product of the human experience, it isn't hard to make the case that this planet is teeming with humans who have forgotten or are struggling to remember they are Souls intrinsically and forever connected to the Universe.

It's an illusion that we are alone or cast aside. It's an illusion that we are separate from the Universe or each other. It's an illusion that we are without higher, divine, spiritual guidance or separate from the loving and guiding force of our Souls. However—and this is key—we've agreed to engage with these illusions. By incarnating here and taking on a human experience, we've decided on a Soul level, to dance with these notions of illusion and to deeply feel, fear, experience, and mistake that we are somehow separate from the Universe and our Souls.

Yep, we all agreed to this. *You* agreed to this.

So, why? Why would we agree to this experience, to forget that we're loved, supported, guided, and held within a much larger sphere of order?

Why?

Well, how else would we learn? How else would we, ultimately and ideally, come to return to our Souls and the Universe, more deeply convinced and embracing of their existence than ever before if we didn't experience separateness? Any great spiritual or mystical thinker or teacher has said as much: it's in the suffering, the illusions, that we find our most significant moments of healing, awareness, and truth. It's when we're on our knees, throwing ourselves at the mercy of the chaotic complication of our human lives that we discover profound simplicity in Universal truths—and, even more importantly, that those truths are contained within us.

Incarnating as a human being sets up a grand walk home. As if we're airdropped somewhere, rough and raw, strange and seemingly unforgiving, tasked with returning home, one sacred and messy step at a time. The journey is supposed to look and feel human: raw, edgy, emotional, fearful, challenged, euphoric, curious, out loud, so that we are continuously inspired and guided (or sometimes forced) to look within and find the truth. *You're here, as a human, this time around, to return to your Soul.*

And the great news is this: while, yes, you've been airdropped, you've also arrived here with all the tools you need to return to your Soul. You've come here already primed and prepped to be successful. You've come here with everything you need to move through your human experiences, to engage with the human illusion of separation, to experience the full expression of your emotional body, and to discover deeply profound and comforting truth within yourself.

Yes, you've been airdropped in what may at times feel like a vast wilderness, but you've come with that beautiful, glorious, comforting Soul tool kit. You've come with intrinsic forces designed to drive you down the right paths; you've come with the capacity to experience and not only survive that experience but to make sense of it and, therefore, of yourself.

Your Soul is your great accompaniment and it's come along ready to talk. Operating in your body as your intuition, your Soul's voice is prepared to guide, pep talk, amplify, nurture, nudge, and reveal truth.

> *Your Soul is your partner, steadfast and constant. Your humanness and all of the experiences within it are your compass, your loving siren call. And your intuition, your deeply held conveyer of truth, is the voice of your Soul.*

Help is never far away. Love never runs dry. Your Soul has come prepared to be an active participant in this journey, and it has positioned you quite well for your trek through the wilderness—for your walk home.

A Message from the Other Side

"Your intuition is your innate reminder that you're a piece of divinity, a spark of conscious energy that is always connected to its highest expression."

Intuition: Getting to Know Your Soul's Voice

As your ultimate partner and guide, your Soul is always available to you. Its voice, your intuition, is constant, though you might sometimes feel very far away from it or worry that you cannot understand its message. Your Soul's voice speaks your language; it understands the ways you process the world around you; it's always chiming in. Your Soul would like you to cultivate and maintain a deep relationship with your intuition so you're engaging in regular, daily conversation with it.

Your intuition is your gut, your seat of knowing, the center of meaningful nagging and persistent inklings. It's always there, always observing and guiding. It's constantly offering you its hand in partnership, guidance, solidarity, and love. Just as your Soul is constant, so is its voice, embedded within you. *Your intuition is your birthright.*

But why intuition? Why not some special teleprompter running across your vision or some deep narrating voice echoing loudly in your mind? Why not some obvious breadcrumb trail so that this whole walk isn't so mysterious?

Well, when you're on the Other Side and in Soul form, there's no language. There's no need for it, actually, because out there, in the Universe, awareness and telepathic knowing are the language. As humans, we use spoken and written language to communicate and relate to each other. In contrast, when we aren't incarnated in physical bodies—when we are simply Souls—we are telepathic.

In Soul form, we transcend language as we currently know it and instead operate within a telepathic system of knowledge and awareness. Therefore, since your Soul's true language is telepathy, you've come in with that. Yes, since you're human, you're engaging with a spoken and written method of communication here in the physical world. But, ultimately, at your core, you're a Soul and, therefore, telepathic. Within your essence, you still live and operate within that system of awareness and knowing.

And so, that telepathic knowing and awareness are right here with you at all times. Being human, though, means you're going to forget it, or become convinced otherwise, or let fear, anxiety, or other intense emotions eclipse, momentarily or longer, your knowledge of this truth. That comes with the territory of being in physical form.

Make no mistake: the constant voice of the Universe within you won't go silent, even if you ignore it, even if you suffer, even if you mess up, fall down, or make mistakes. No one and nothing can take it from you. Your intuition is your personal, direct line to your Soul, and it will brilliantly magnify when you choose to embrace it.

SACRED INTENTION-SETTING:
Discovering the Seat of Your Intuition

As your Soul's voice, your intuition is a sacred tool and gift. It is always with you and responds faithfully when consulted, listened to, and honored. Let's get you more deeply acquainted with your intuition and discover where in your body your intuition sits or lives. For each of us this is different, but have no doubt: your intuition resides within you.

When you're ready, read silently or aloud this intention:

I open with curiosity and love to my Soul's voice. I welcome awareness of what my seat of intuition looks like and where in my body it resides. I imagine how this seat of intuition looks and how welcoming and perfectly comfortable it is. I welcome a physical sensation, an awareness, or a directive word or phrase, to help me identify where in my body my seat of intuition resides.

As I discover where in my body my intuition sits, I ease into a greater understanding of it. I open and allow myself to notice what this seat of intuition looks like in greater detail. I notice the colors and the nature of the energy in and around it. I notice the weight of it, whether it's solid and heavy, or light and airy. I notice any movement or flow. I notice how my intuition lives and breathes. I notice what it feels like when I sit in this seat of wisdom and how my body responds when I settle into this space that holds me.

I bless this place with gratitude, love, and care. I extend to my seat of intuition my sincere appreciation and openness to working more readily with it.

I intend to deepen my practice of tuning in, paying attention, listening, and responding to my Soul's voice. I know that I can visualize my seat of intuition and settle into it at any time, as often as I would like.

 POWERING INTENTION WITH ACTION

Consider what supportive action steps you might take to become familiar with your Soul's voice and with this seat of your intuition. Perhaps you might begin a practice wherein each morning, upon waking, you settle into your seat of intuition and ask it, *"What is most important for me today?"* or *"How might I take good, loving care of myself today?"* or *"What message do I need to take in at this time?"* Or, you might set aside a few minutes each day to become quiet and centered, and simply come to the seat of your intuition to observe. Remember the value of supportive, single strides: this is a relationship you're building, and with frequency and trust, it will grow.

Building a Relationship
with Your Intuition

Intuition is your birthright. It isn't a special thing that some people have and some people don't have; we all have it. It's our relationship with our intuition that varies.

No matter your current relationship with your intuition, begin with acceptance. Be in recognition of this sacred gift. Accept that you have fully functioning intuition; that it's whole, it's unique to you, and it's your Soul's voice. Accept and then allow that this intuition is yours to reclaim, discover, uncover, remember, embrace, use, grow, explore, make personal, and integrate into your life. Your intuition is working within the grand Universal framework of telepathy, knowledge, and awareness. It's one of your Soul's most sacred tools, and it's a gift to you.

If you've already accepted and embraced your intuition, and perhaps have a nice working relationship with your intuition, then allow yourself to go deeper, and to trust and engage with it even more. Each of us can always live our lives more intuitively. There is always room to go deeper, reach greater authenticity, and find new truth.

Ask yourself: What would it look like for me to deepen my relationship with my intuition? What feels like the next right step on my path to growing my relationship with my intuition? Is there another way I might accept more deeply the gift of my intuition and allow it in my life?

Next, it's vitally important to understand that, like every spiritual truth, there is a component of personal responsibility. That is, to make magic, you have to wave the wand. Or at least recite the incantation. The Universe does its best work when we meet it halfway, when we use our personal power to participate and take intentional, self-initiated steps on our walk home.

It's crucial to take responsibility for your relationship with your intuition because taking responsibility activates the power of choice—and there's nothing your intuition loves more than being welcomed into your life and acted upon.

SACRED INTENTION-SETTING:

Accepting and Taking Responsibility
for Your Intuition

Your intuition is yours to grow, amplify, and strengthen. It's your tool to pick up and use. It's yours to use to alleviate your suffering, to make sense of your confusion, to illuminate your next steps, to clarify what's right and true for you. It's yours to consult with, listen to, consider, and trust. Whether you're new to your intuition or seasoned in working with it, there is always room to go deeper and align further with your Soul's voice. Let's set an intention to accept the gift of your intuition, to take responsibility for your relationship with it, and to take that next step in growing your intuition, whatever that is for you.

When you're ready, read silently or aloud this intention:

I accept and embrace my intuition and the sacred connection to my Soul it offers me. I welcome responsibility for my part in the relationship with my intuition. I open to and welcome the loving guiding force my intuition provides. I invite any potential blocks to accessing my intuition to arise so that I may honor, understand, heal, and release them. I welcome deeper alignment with my Soul's voice and embrace my part in strengthening that sacred and loving connection.

POWERING INTENTION WITH ACTION

Consider what supportive action steps you might take in accepting, taking responsibility for, and choosing a relationship with your intuition. Perhaps think of, in this instance, your intuition as a small child or an animal you love deeply. How might you build trust, responsiveness, and engagement? How might you take responsibility for your part in the relationship, carry yourself, and treat the one you love? How might acceptance and responsibility deepen trust, faith, and safety within the relationship?

Your Conversational Intuition

Your intuition is like a muscle; it builds and gains strength the more you use it and rely on it. Your Soul uses your intuition to help you, to send you clues and insights, to prompt and spur you, to offer reassurance and compassion, and to remind you that magic, guidance, and divine synchronicities are commonplace on this human journey.

Your power to strengthen your intuition comes in regarding your relationship with it as a two-way street whereby you welcome information and insights and are willing to respond to what you receive.

Your intuition is your Soul's supportive, conversational voice. It wants to have regular, ongoing conversations with you. In fact, your Soul would love for your daily life to become an intuitive conversation! That's how ready it is to talk to you and engage with you.

The primary pivot point in building your relationship with your intuition is the art of conversation: listening and responding. If you're on board with taking responsibility for your part (listening and responding) of building a relationship with your intuition, then that naturally leads you to a place of choice.

Choosing to listen to and receive what your Soul's voice is offering you is momentous; it's the beginning of taking something that's inside of you and translating it into your outer world. When, upon listening and receiving, you choose to respond, you're bringing human consciousness to the insight of your Soul. That is: you're going in, to listen and receive, so that you can then go out, responding to and taking action on behalf of what your Soul has presented to you.

You're activating your intuition when you faithfully listen, receive, respond, and then allow it to influence your human life.

As we talk about having a conversational relationship with your intuition, you might wonder just how out loud this conversation needs to become. Know that there is a lot of freedom in how you may choose or prefer to develop this.

For some, speaking out loud—very literally out loud—is helpful. You might find that when you receive a little nudge or piece of guidance that responding out loud helps bring that information to a more concrete, aware place. Sometimes speaking out loud in response to your Soul's voice enables you to consider an idea, a bit like kneading and forming dough, taking something that might not feel totally clear or formed and making it more accessible and workable. You might even discover that the more you engage in an out-loud conversation with your intuition, the more you perceive its responses, and in that back-and-forth, arrive at a place of inspiration, clarity, or readiness to take action.

Alternatively, you might be someone who prefers to receive and consider messages quietly, holding that conversation within your being and responding in an almost telepathic way. Many people experience their intuition as a conversation in their head and find that more inward-focused process helpful. They can feel the power of what's building within them and come to know or settle deeply into the guidance offered.

It's important to remember, too, that intuition often comes as an awareness. It can feel very much like a deep knowing that simply arrives in your being. As such, it might come with a physical sensation: a body chill, flutter in your stomach, or a tug in your chest. Notice if you experience physical sensations when you receive intuitive messages and, over time, place your trust in those bodily notes. You can have a conversation with these physical sensations as well.

Ultimately, the advice to engage in and build a conversational relationship with your intuition offers you plenty of room to determine just what that looks like for you. Do what feels right and feels most helpful.

Do not, however, stop doing something that feels right and helpful because you worry people will think you're crazy. Don't hold back because you worry you're making it up, or you're concerned you're just thinking about what you wish would happen, or you're afraid of what your spouse would think of you. That's your human mind getting in the way. Use the conversation with your intuition as a tool to bypass that human hang-up and step into relationship with your Soul. Push aside that old thought pattern in your head with the action of conversation—you'll create a new way of operating.

The power of your intuitive voice comes alive when it becomes a conversation that moves you, shifts you, and spurs action. This conversation is the process of taking something mystical, sacred, divine, and impossible to hold and translating it into something practical, doable, relatable, and very possible to hold.

Intuition Arrives Without Emotion

Intuition has its own hallmarks—typical ways of showing up or operating—that are consistent and helpful.

Chief among these hallmarks is that intuition arrives without emotion. True, pristine intuitive guidance doesn't come wrapped in fear or worry or some other intense emotion. No, real intuition comes without emotion, often arriving packaged as a simple sentence, awareness, or knowledge. The truth doesn't have an opinion about itself—it's just the truth. So when it arrives in your being, it will show up as a knowing awareness.

Sure, you might react emotionally in the moments after receiving the message (*"What? I can't do that, that's crazy!"* or *"Wow, that's a little bit scary, I wonder how I'd make that change?"* or *"Oh my gosh! If that happened, it would be wonderful! I'd feel so relieved!"*), but that initial arrival of the intuitive hit is usually clean, clear, pure—without human emotion. The awareness that arrives, if you're tuning into it, will feel like it brings a gravity with it. It won't feel chaotic or fervent or wild; it'll feel quiet, reliable, intentioned, and sacred.

Remember: you know the truth by the way it feels.

See if you can begin to perceive the difference between the intuitive information and your follow-up reaction to it, and then, see if you can lengthen the space between receiving that information and your reaction. Try to create a sacred pause around the arrival of intuitive guidance, letting it be for a while before your human mind gets ahold of it. This can be tough, and it takes practice, but it will help you separate Soul guidance from your human ego, fears, and narratives.

Creating and cultivating a practice of receiving and then pausing around your intuition will help you bypass your human reactions and settle more knowingly into this intuitive, divine, Soul-inspired space.

Self-Trust and Self-Love: The Gifts of Your Intuition

Your intuition wants nothing more than to inspire you to shift, move, grow, advance, learn, and heal. Its entire purpose is to be the voice of your Soul and your greatest ally. It loves little more than spurring you to take some kind of action. And, when you do so, not only will you have strengthened your relationship with your intuition, you'll have strengthened your relationship with yourself.

In trusting your intuition—and in believing it so fiercely that you allow it to guide your footsteps—you're building deep self-trust. When you listen to what's being communicated to you from deep within your being, when you accept and embrace those messages, and then, when you translate those messages into action, you've found a recipe for evolution, awakening, and self-love.

Your intuition will help you get to know yourself, what's best for you, your path, and your truth. When you're living in conversation with it, it'll provide you comfort, support, and reassurance that you're not alone.

With your intuition, you'll feel more connected to divine guidance, trusting of yourself, safe, and at ease.

Living in accordance with your intuition is perhaps the most direct path to self-love. There is nothing that validates your Soul, value, and worth, like allowing the sacredness of your intuition to guide your life.

Taking Action: Unlocking the Power of Your Intuition

Your intuition strengthens and becomes more apparent to you as you take it seriously, listen closely and, within the best of your ability, do what it's asking of you. Ultimately, you unlock the sacred power and profound gifts of your intuition when you listen to and receive what's been communicated to you and then pair it with action.

Taking action is the golden rule of intuition development. It's the essential core of your intuitive power. It's where all of the transformation, evolution, awakening, and conscious growth lie.

And, as is often the case with profound and sacred Universal Truths, the "simple" task of pairing your intuition with action can become complicated, frustrating, challenging, even heart-wrenching.

Remember: it's usually only after we've encountered our blocks, resistance, deep-seated fears, and raw emotional content around these sacred lessons that we come upon the profound simplicity inherent in them. That is, engaging with sacred truths often feels like a raw, emotional, chaotic mess at first (and often in the middle), well before we arrive at the gifts they give us. So, be patient with yourself, go easy on yourself, and don't take personally the difficulty that might come up here.

It's normal that your intuition will offer guidance that's relatively easy to follow: take a left at the intersection ahead, send a card to your mom, check in with your boss before you leave for the day, read the spiritual book you've seen pop up in your social media feeds for the last month.

It's also typical that your intuition will offer guidance that is incredibly inconvenient to follow—the kind of guidance that, if followed, will change your life and require you to act in spite of fear. Release an old friendship that no longer offers support, end your marriage or long-term relationship, pull your child out of public school and find the right specialized education setting, change your job, take a leap to start your own business—this is the kind of guidance that prompts most of us, at one time or another, to ignore or push aside our intuition.

So, yes, pairing your intuition with action can be far more complicated than it sounds. That's okay. There's, frankly, no getting around it, though. For right now, at this moment, you're simply being asked to accept and sit with this truth: *taking action based upon intuitive guidance is one of the most effective and profound ways to live a life inspired by your Soul.*

Breaking It Down: What Kind of Action Does Your Intuition Require?

So, what kind of action does your intuition require of you? First, let's set the stage: since your intuition is your Soul and its voice, it's inherently kind. It's understanding, compassionate, thoughtful, and loving. It's divinely supportive, supremely wise, and won't let you down. It's also determined, clear, unequivocal, and at times, demanding. It wants the very best for you; it wants to assist you in aligning with your Soul and living your human life from that place.

Your intuition also knows the value of an action step, no matter how small that step seems. It recognizes the importance of a shifted perspective, a willingness to consider new ideas, and the ah-ha moment. And sometimes, that's the extent of what it's asking you for: to simply engage with a new idea or consider something in a way you haven't before. Sometimes, your intuition simply wants you to awaken to a new paradigm or notion. To simply receive it, look at it, consider it and say, *"Huh, interesting."*

Sometimes, the small prompts from your intuition will feel doable: take the long way home from work, speak up (or perhaps don't speak up) in the meeting, pick up the phone rather than let it go to voicemail, say *"yes"* (or *"no"*) to the opportunity being offered to you, join a yoga class, try a guided meditation, read that book, don't go to that party because you need to stay in and rest.

These small prompts often feel like they make really good sense and, for the most part, are socially acceptable and personally doable. Don't underestimate them, though. Do you know how many people ignore these? How many people routinely say, *"Ahh, I should have,"* or *"I knew I shouldn't have…"*?

There's a cost to not listening to these small prompts. The cost is this: when you don't respond and pair with action these more minor prompts, you're missing easily accessed opportunities to build your relationship with your intuition, and you're losing valuable moments within which to gain self-trust.

Responding to these small prompts with confident action is an immediate trust-builder between you and your intuition. These small wins build a strong foundation that you'll come to rely upon over time, and, especially, when life is more complicated and the guidance more life-changing.

These smaller intuitive hits are also the ones that build your self-care routine, strengthen your courage and willingness to love and honor yourself and keep you emotionally, spiritually, physically, and mentally safe and nourished. They're the places to practice these things and, for the most part, gather some wins. And that just feels good, all around. You've listened and responded to your intuition, thereby strengthening it, and you've taken good care of yourself, even loved yourself, thus increasing your self-trust.

It feels awfully good, awfully satisfying, awfully congruent to live intuitively, doesn't it?

Good! Keep doing it! Keep listening to those smaller bits of guidance! Momentum, when it comes to living a spiritual and intuitive life, is like that best friend who sometimes knows you better than you know yourself.

SACRED INTENTION-SETTING:

Connecting with Your Intuition's Small Prompts
and Actionable Guidance

Collecting some smaller, easily actionable pieces of guidance is a great way to engage with and practice using your
intuition. It builds that intuitive muscle, cultivates self-
trust, and provides you with ready-made opportunities to
translate inner guidance into your waking, walking, daily
human life.

When you're ready, read silently or aloud this intention:

*With intention and curiosity, I arrive at the seat of my intu-
ition. This familiar place is nourishing and comforting. I know
this place. Here, I open to my intuition and ask that it share with
me small prompts, doable actions, and accessible truths that I
can translate into my life with ease.*

*I welcome the experience of receiving insight, listening to
what's shared with me, and then responding to it with a commitment to take action. I welcome the insights that I might readily recognize and translate into action. I trust myself to receive
what comes, to allow my doubts to rise and then release as I
embrace what's revealed to me.*

*I feel the experience of receiving insight that I know is true
for me. I feel myself accepting that insight. I consider ways to*

translate that insight into my conscious life. I feel and extend gratitude to my intuition for its clarity and to myself to trusting my Soul's voice.

POWERING INTENTION WITH ACTION

What did you receive in that process? What came up? What did your intuition show you, ask you, reveal to you? Breathe into that. Listen, accept, receive, and then...pair it with action.

When Taking Action Feels Daunting

The lighter intuitive hits feel nice, don't they? They may feel familiar, as if you've just gotten clarity about a message that's been nagging you for some time. These smaller prompts feel doable and even exciting or relief-giving.

Good. Feel them. Follow through on them. Build that muscle and practice. Trust yourself and your Soul's voice. You deserve this.

And, you'll be grateful that you've allowed yourself to engage with your intuition in this way because it will support you—it'll build that foundation—when the insight and accompanying process aren't so light.

There are times when your intuitive guidance will feel heavier, more intensive, perhaps even daunting. It might stop you in your tracks with the inconvenient and disruptive nature of its truth: change your job, end your marriage, overhaul your eating habits, set healthy boundaries with friends, stop engaging with a toxic family member, follow your lifelong dream, take a leap.

Sometimes, the guidance isn't an easy check mark on the to-do list. Sometimes, the guidance carries a solemnity with it, a seriousness that you know will create profound and permanent change in your life. Sometimes, you know that accepting intuitive guidance means accepting a truth you've been avoiding for some time, and acting on that guidance will bring you to a new place—a place there's no coming back from.

These moments are when your relationship with your intuition can become much more complicated and even tested. This is when many people back off, push it down or aside, opting, understandably, to keep their lives the same, comfortable, for just a little longer. This is when our fears of change, loss, release, and the unknown grip our ankles and stop us cold. This is when we discount, diminish, and ignore our intuition, or engage in behaviors to numb the intuitive nagging.

As you know (and you do know), engaging with your life in a spiritual way places demands upon you. And the more you rise to meet those demands—and collect the growth and enlightenment that come with them—the more you'll be asked to live honestly. The honesty we're talking about here is one that you feel in your bones, to your core, right to your Soul. It's an honesty that prevents you from lying to yourself. It's an honesty that almost inherently requires bravery and courage.

And so, this is also why it can be awfully attractive to disconnect from our intuition: we know, to our core, that the more we listen, respond, engage, and take action, the more we'll face profound, life-changing truth. And that truth will become nearly impossible to ignore.

We can handily make excuses, usually about the lack of time, money, support, or resources, that enable us to set aside what we intuitively know to be accurate and return to a state of comfort and safety. Or, we can outright disconnect from that intuitive voice, refusing to allow it air time.

How do we deal with this disconnection when we feel it coming up? Practice. Take the small steps. When in doubt, acknowledge and honor what's been communicated to you. You don't need to change your life overnight; simply take the step of admitting truth, especially the inconvenient and uncomfortable truth, to yourself.

Sometimes, when things are tougher and more intense, your intuition simply wants you to acknowledge the truth. Sometimes that acknowledgment is, for the time being, the action step. Allow yourself space when the right step is simply sitting with the difficult truth your intuition has revealed.

For instance, you might know that a relationship in your life must come to an end. You've consulted with your intuition, and sure enough, all that deep knowing and nagging has come from within. It's true. You know it. And it's terrifying. *What about the money? What about a place to live? What about all those years together? What will my family and friends say? What will their family and friends say? Will I be alone afterward? What if I'm alone for the rest of my life? How can I do this to them? What about the kids? I'm scared. I know it's true, but I am afraid.*

This is a terrifying place. It's why so many people ignore or numb out their intuition. It can bring us to our knees to live our lives spiritually, connected to our Souls and our intuition. Inconvenient truth? That's an understatement.

This example helps us see that an appropriate first action step might simply be to acknowledge the truth that's come up. You'd never want to charge headlong into this kind of change without process, consideration, planning, and getting in deep touch with your center. And so, sometimes action is accepting what's been revealed to you, acknowledging that this incredibly difficult truth resonates with you.

And yes, it will require action down the road. It will. But first steps first. Be kind to yourself.

It's worth noting here that your intuition loves a project. That is: in making significant life-changing shifts, your intuition prefers you take things a step at a time. It likes to be consulted at each of those junctures and will offer you guidance and insight specific to what's happening in that moment, at that crossroads. *Breaking down significant change into doable pieces, even if emotional and hard, is an approach your intuition will embrace.*

The thing is, your intuition—your Soul—won't abandon you, especially when you've engaged with the process of shifting your life in a brave, truth-based way.

Your intuition knows that leaps take faith, change comes with fear, and that living a life congruent with the Soul requires bravery and courage.

Your intuition will be right there with you each step of the way. It won't stop revealing to you what's more authentic, more healthy, more whole, more supportive of and for you. It won't stop nosing you down the spiritual path where you'll find the most important truths about yourself. It won't stop being patient with you when you need to catch your breath, grieve, or process. Your Soul and its voice are loyal companions on the journey, particularly when times get tough.

 ## SACRED INTENTION-SETTING:

Connecting with Your Intuition When Faced with Daunting Truth

---

If this is a time and space that's right for you to take a look at a deeper, perhaps more daunting issue in your life, then this intention exercise is for you. If this isn't the time or place for that, that's just fine, and you can move to the next section. Remember: you can always come back to this intention when you're ready to do so.

When you're ready, read silently or aloud this intention:

I arrive at my seat of intuition with openness and willingness. As I consider (state your concern/problem/issue), I welcome insight and guidance. As I experience the emotional content

of this situation and consider the emotional content to come, I welcome insight from my Soul about what the next right step might be and how I might take sacred care of myself in that step. As this situation is complicated and even overwhelming, I welcome insight into a specific area or detail I should focus on at this time. I welcome insight into where my focus is most needed and my energy best spent at this time. I trust myself to receive what's in my Highest and Best Honor, and, even when difficult, I trust myself to take action that is aligned with truth and self-awareness.

**POWERING INTENTION
WITH ACTION**

This takes courage, to look at a deep, painful, life-changing truth. Consider what is before you at this time: Accepting a truth first? Do you need to sit with an awareness you've been ignoring? Do you need time to spend with a truth that causes you grief or pain? Or, maybe, it's time to take a small action step? How might you take good care of yourself at this time and through this process? What brave truth do you need to admit to yourself right now?

The Courageous, Intuitive Life

When we're steeped in the human experience, struggling in a time of significant loss, stressed about money, our children, our aging parents, or our jobs, it can become so easy to lose touch with our intuition.

Even in times when we aren't experiencing outright suffering, most of us are living within structures and societies where embracing our spiritual nature and building a life according to our intuition is an act of defiance. So many of our humanly created systems—government, political, religious, educational, even our family systems—are built upon (and rely upon) individuals ignoring their intuitive voices and instead allowing the rules, expectations, and momentum of the system to direct us.

In many cases, there have been system-wide attacks on personal spiritual practice and people who live their lives intuitively. People who acknowledge the spiritual nature of their lives have been maligned, bullied, or rejected. We live in a society that prefers we look outside of ourselves for direction and guidance. It's a society whose capitalistic structure doesn't make anyone money if you're listening to your internal voice rather than outside voices of influence.

And so, in our society, it's an act of radical defiance to embrace your personal power and live by your intuition. It's an act of defiance to resist conditioning and expectations so you can live what you know is right. You risk rejection and being branded the black sheep in your family when you dare to throw off generations of conditioning and expectation in favor of finding and building your life around a deeper, more resonant, personal truth.

Your conditioned human brain will tell you you've made up the messages your intuition sends you; it'll tell you you're crazy or silly or warn you that people in your life would laugh if they knew what you were doing. Your conditioned humanness will tell you you can't trust what you've heard or received, and certainly, that it's better to stay right where you are, all comfy and status quo-ish, rather than follow some slightly perceived, foggy nudge.

Do not feel ashamed. You are not bad. You are not crazy. You are not disloyal. You are not disrespectful of history, tradition, your elders, your parents, long-standing institutions, or what came before you. You are brave and courageous to stand up against the forces in your life that pressure you to conform or to be less powerful or to forget that truth is found within.

That you are willing to release belonging, groupthink, and the pressure of our society is triumphant. That you are eager to reclaim, defiantly if necessary, your Soul and your most authentic self, is triumphant.

The beauty of accepting, listening to, and pairing your intuition with action is that doing this, repeatedly, builds profound self-trust. You will come to know yourself more deeply than ever before. You will come to trust yourself more deeply and surely than you ever have. Engaging with your intuition, welcoming its conversational nature, and embracing its guidance builds a deep-seated self-trust. From here, it's much easier to identify what's true for you and live in alignment with your Soul.

Living intuitively means that you find your truth inside of you rather than outside of you.

It takes bravery and courage to accept your intuition. Even more to listen to it. And more still to pair it with action. But this is why you're here. You're here to do the things that require grit-your-teeth bravery and oh-screw-it courage. You're here to receive the gifts of your Soul and to build a human life that feels vibrant, true, congruent, and full.

BREAKING IT DOWN

- Your intuition is your Soul's voice, always talking to you. Accept this truth and engage in a conversational relationship with your intuition.

- Listen and respond to the messages your intuition gives you and then pair those intuitive messages with action, whether small or large.

- Remember that intuitive messages often come as a deep awareness, sometimes with a physical sensation, and without human emotion. See if you can create a sacred pause around these moments before your human mind takes over.

- Understand that your conditioning, religion, parents, family, society, gender roles, habits, fears, cultures, and traditions may send you messages that your intuition does not exist or is wayward. Understand this and give yourself permission to release it.

- Take single, intentioned, brave steps. No matter what.

- Be courageous and know: it can be a radical act of defiance to live according to your intuition, and not everyone will understand it, but that courageousness will help you build a human life that is congruent and in alignment with your Soul.

A Message from the Other Side

"Sometimes your intuition knows—your whole body knows—well before your mind accepts what is true, what you must do. Often, a leap of faith is required to follow your truth. You'll need to find your courageous inner core to do what you know is right and true for you. You'll need to remember that your intuition is a reminder that faith is rewarded. Courage and faith will always exist alongside fear. You must allow the force of self-love to outweigh the force of fear. Your intuition has been given to you to help you do this."

"Do not assume that divine guidance flows only when you are in need of help. Guidance continues to flow whether or not you have problems. It transcends problems, heartbreaks, and traumas, flowing through dreams and illuminations. Whether guidance comes during times of tranquility or trauma, however, it is up to you to have the courage to acknowledge it."

—Caroline Myss, *Entering The Castle*

-- ♥ --

"Joy is the infallible sign of the presence of God."

—Pierre Teilhard de Chardin

Chapter Three

Divine Guidance Is Always Available

You are a Soul, and therefore you are divine. No matter what happens in this human form, the constant, perennial truth is that *you are a piece of divinity expressing itself in the Universe.* Therefore, you always—always—have access to divine support, guidance, intervention, inspiration, and love. Guidance is constant; believing in and engaging with it grants you deeper, more precise alignment with your Soul.

The Universe and its divine forces are kind, friendly, and loving. They also teach lessons, restore everything to balance (one way or another, over time), and march, always, to the drumbeat of evolution. Ultimately, because our Souls are part and parcel of the Universe, we have access to all the ways the Universe affirms and confirms that we are loved, valuable, worthy, ever-evolving, and sacredly important.

The Universe is unconditionally loving, and its forces are our allies, encouraging us to deepen our connections to our spiritual center. Chief among these loyal, friendly, and unwaveringly helpful Universal forces is our Spirit Team—the team of Souls, divine guides, angels, and others who journey with us and offer loving guidance and support along the way.

The Anatomy of Guidance

From the humans you've lived with who have crossed over to Spirit Guides that watch over you and assist your Soul, each of us has a divine team and direct connection to them. While your intuition, as your Soul's voice, comes from within you, this kind of spiritual guidance, from spiritual beings and other Souls, comes from outside of you. You will often feel their impact within your body and energetically, though they are uniquely different from your own intuition. Your Spirit Team offers its own distinct, steady, sacred, and loving guiding voice.

Your divine guides, as your Spirit Team, are enthusiastic and steadfast in their desire to show you the way to your Soul.

Ideally, you'll find that the guidance offered by your Spirit Guides echoes your intuition, or that one force amplifies the other. This is the brilliance of the tools of your Soul: when used and accessed together, they magnify, clarify, and amplify each other.

The Spirit Team

Each of us has our own Spirit Team. It's a team of Souls, guides, and loving forces that support us, offering assistance and insight on our journeys. Of course, as is the case with our intuition, we must establish, use, and grow our connections with our Spirit Team. It's our human doubts and fears that most often cause us to question the existence or presence of our Spirit Team. And so, just as with our intuition, we have a role to play in moving through our doubts, fears, and blocks, allowing ourselves to step fully into this divinely helpful connection.

The great news is that every time you move through fear or break through a period of doubt and come into more profound connection with your Spirit Team, you feel, sense, perceive, or become aware of their presence more clearly.

They are always with you. They interact with you in different ways, sending signs or signals, meeting up with you in your dream state, or conspiring to create serendipitous circumstances in your life. Like your Soul and your intuition, your Spirit Team is steadfast and constant. These tools of the Soul offer divine proof that you are not alone.

Loved Ones on the Other Side

When the humans you've journeyed with in this lifetime pass away, their Souls return to the Other Side. Their paths to the Other Side are varied and individual, depending on what they need to heal, understand, and learn. Souls often experience a period of rest upon returning to the Other Side, going through a kind of incubation and rejuvenation. This rest period allows the Soul to disconnect from the human identity and experience (so that it may later be reviewed, understood, and healed) and to reconnect to the vast, expansive, rejuvenating Universal forces on the Other Side.

This rest period can last for varying amounts of "time," depending on how arduous the Soul's human life was. (Here, "time" is in quotes because, on the Other Side, time as we humans know it does not exist. Time is a human construct.) Some Souls require greater incubation and rejuvenation periods because of a particularly tumultuous human life, while others might move through that rest period relatively quickly.

From there, a Soul will engage in a life review, understanding what they experienced in human form and participating in any necessary healing. This is where karmic forces come into play, as a Soul might need to understand that there is something they did in their human lifetime or a lesson they did not learn or embody, that needs, essentially, to be balanced out. Rather than a strict "payback" system, karma simply asks Souls to build empathy, understanding, and personal responsibility for what has occurred. Sometimes this is a more straightforward feat; other times, this is profoundly complicated or intense.

Just like the rest period, a Soul's time in this life review and healing and balancing process varies. A Soul's journey continues well after passing from human form and onto the Other Side; growth, healing, consciousness-raising, and evolution exist here and there, and march forward, with love and steadfastness.

By and large, the Souls who come through in psychic or mediumship readings or connect with you in dreams, visitations, or through intuitive awareness are participating in this process of understanding, healing, balancing, and clearing.

Souls on the Other Side want you to have access to a greater perspective on your human life and hopefully, to shed layers of suffering, disillusionment, and wounding, so that you become more joyful, present, and connected to your Soul.

They want to join with you to heal and grow, atone and evolve, transcend, and understand human experiences and lessons. Souls on the Other Side, for the most part, want to contribute to your growth and evolution, offering you gifts and profound insights from their "new" perspective.

Souls on the Other Side want to remind you that the Other Side exists! That Souls don't die! They want you to remember that you are safe, guided, and held. They want you to remember that there is always—always—a larger plan that is loving and kind. They want you to take heart, have faith, and feel love. They want you to take a break from taking life so seriously, to step out of the intensity of your head and your personal narratives, and find relief in the vastness of the divine. They want you to remember that you're never alone, that you're looked after, and that the walking of your path is of divine importance. They want you to laugh, release, feel, and be comforted.

The Souls of those you love show up in the words or an embrace of a kind friend, in the song lyrics that jump out of your radio the moment you turn your car on, or in flowers of a certain type or color. These Souls arrive as the pair of cardinals in your backyard or prompt knowing laughter when you find the penny they've left for you.

They'll drop Christmas ornaments from your tree or break grandma's old ceramic bowl (relax, they're trying to make you laugh!); they'll flatten your car tire to make you late for the appointment so that you encounter a different doctor (the right doctor!); they'll flash lights, mess with the water pressure in the shower, and send you repeating numbers. It's as if they're asking you, *"Do you believe me now?"*

The family heirlooms and treasured passed-down pocket watches, antique jewelry, or sentimental tokens are powerful. Because they mean so much to you, your loved ones on the Other Side will use these material objects like portals. They'll connect with you, sending you energy or messages or comfort when you wear or carry or treasure these objects. They have power and weight because they mean so much to you, making them ideal tools for your loved ones to use to connect with you.

Please know your connection with your loved ones doesn't diminish in any way should these objects become lost or passed on to someone else. You won't disappoint or anger them should material objects come or go; they'll simply find other ways to connect with you.

There are entire books written exclusively about signs from your human loved ones who've crossed over. And rightfully so! These connections are profoundly important and transcendent.

> *The connections to our loved ones on the Other Side are meant to teach us and heal us, granting us the kind of reassurance and faith that encourages us forward on our Soul journeys.*

Think of your loved ones on the Other Side as essential allies and assets on your Spirit Team. Your connection to them remains, and if you allow it, this connection offers opportunities for you to heal, grow, evolve, and transcend the limitations of the human mind and experience.

These Souls on the Other Side have access to something that, admittedly, is harder for us because we're human: they have access to the big picture, to the map of our Souls, and our plans for evolution and growth. If you listen, they'll bring these things to you. They want you to remember them; they want to add illumination, clarity, and light to your path and your steps. They want to remind you that there is something much, much larger—

and much more spiritual—going on. They want to grant you the comfort and nourishment of that truth.

Your loved ones want you to keep going, knowing that there is, categorically, a point to all of this. They know this more than ever when they die and return to Soul form. These loving Soul partners want you to stay close to your Soul and to remember that you are a human on Earth so that you can walk this spiritual path of self-discovery. Keep moving, keep being brave, knowing that you're loved and never alone.

When the Human Relationship Leaves Wounds

There may be Souls on the Other Side with whom you had difficulty. You may not feel loving, friendly, or welcoming toward some of the people you've known who have passed away. You may even feel a sense of "good riddance" or that you're now much safer with the passing of this human being. That's okay. *Yes, that is okay.*

The truth is that many of us have abusive people in our lives, right in our families of origin and intimate circles, and we are safer when these people are no longer with us. By no means is there an expectation or requirement that you martyr the dead—in fact, please don't!

If there has been someone in your life whose impact on you has been traumatizing, wounding, and hurtful, you must honor this. Death doesn't erase what a human has done in their lifetime; death doesn't indemnify someone from the wounding they caused another. Therefore, in no way must you absolve someone from what they've done to you simply because they've passed away. Instead, it's essential that you honor what's happened and treat yourself with loving kindness and take the steps necessary to heal and care for yourself. The residual impact of these experiences is real and needs to be addressed safely and supportively.

When these Souls cross over, an automatic process of evolution takes place, powered by the Universe's intention to heal and make whole what has become wounded or separate. Sometimes, this process is extensive, and as a result, your interaction with that Soul might be limited or nonexistent.

Other times, Souls will reach out to those they've hurt in their human lives, visiting in dreams or offering a sense of their presence at a family member's home or in a psychic mediumship reading. Souls do come forward offering apology and regret, often in their process of taking responsibility for the hurt they've caused.

Still, you can determine where you are in your own healing process and just how closely you'd like to align or work with that Soul. It might never feel safe or right to welcome a particular Soul into your life as a guide, and that is okay. Just as in life, setting boundaries in death is an important self-care tool.

It is also possible that a hard human relationship might undergo a profound transformation when someone passes away and returns to Soul form. You might feel connections or visitations that heal you, release emotions, clear old wounds, and bring about natural understanding or forgiveness. Those cycles of shifting or even spontaneous healing often occur, and you'll know them by how right, true, and complete they feel.

Ultimately, you have the right to determine what feels safe and correct for you when it comes to connecting with Souls on the Other Side.

There is no pressure to suddenly forgive and forget or to keep quiet about what it was like to be in relationship with them. The only way to heal something is to tell yourself the truth about it, feel it, and honor it. Sometimes, a death offers the shifting necessary for you to heal or overcome a painful human experience, and it's important that you allow for this.

In working practically within this situation, a helpful tool is intention-setting. For instance, in opening up to your Spirit Guides, you can ask that only those in your *Highest and Best Honor* come forward. Or, if you feel the presence of a loved one on the Other Side with whom you had a troubled relationship, and you're unsure if you should further a connection, you could consult with your intuition, asking, *"Is this Soul here in accordance with my Highest and Best Honor?"* If the answer is no, tell that Soul to move along. If the answer is yes, you can decide if you'd like to allow yourself to connect to the Soul. You could also say, if you're unclear about receiving an answer, *"If this Soul is not in my Highest and Best Honor, I request that it move along."*

You have the power to take control of the spiritual situation and do what feels right for you, at that moment. Remember, you are the seat of your power and it is your right to determine what feels safe and true for you.

Sometimes, resolution with someone is just not possible, even in death. Still, you can always—always—love yourself enough to find your version of peaceful resolution so that you aren't suffering.

SACRED INTENTION-SETTING:
Connecting with Your Loved Ones
on the Other Side

As we pause to set a sacred intention around connecting with your loved ones on the Other Side, close your eyes and ask your body: What would it feel like to house, cradle, and nurture the connection to your loved ones? Where in your body would this connection like to live? Notice any physical sensation that comes up or if your awareness is directed to a certain area of your body. Notice if you receive a word (*"heart"*) or directive (*"within your second chakra"*). The space or place within your body that comes to your awareness, in whatever way, is the place where the seat of connection with your loved ones' Souls would like to live.

When you're ready, read silently or aloud this intention:

I welcome discovering and deepening my connections with my loved ones on the Other Side. I appreciate those Souls who have offerings, guidance, and contributions that are in my Highest and Best Honor. I welcome healing, forgiveness, and karma-clearing that is occurring on the Other Side, with Souls connected to me, that is in my Highest and Best Honor. I embrace and allow the love, guidance, safety, support, comfort, insight, and growth

that is mine to receive. I will treat myself kindly and with com-
passion as I learn to experience, discern, understand, and take
in the guidance from my loved ones' Souls. I allow this seat of
connection to grow, root, and flourish in my being.

 POWERING INTENTION
WITH ACTION

What is one action step you could take today to
strengthen your intuitive connections with your loved
ones on the Other Side? What sign or signal might you
honor or embrace? What fear or anxiety might you allow to lessen or dissolve to more deeply accept, believe, and know that you are connected to your loved
ones' Souls?

Spirit Guides

Our Spirit Team has other members, alongside these
humans who've crossed over. While many of us look to
these more familiar Souls for comfort, we each have Spirit
Guides who operate at a high, overarching level and have
profound gifts to offer.

These Spirit Guides reside beyond our earthly plane,
offering us connection to what often feels mystical or

otherworldly. Our experiences of them are varied: some people have a deep awareness of a tribe of Native Americans; some have received long, intensive moments of eye contact with indigenous beings tending to a fire in a cave; others have seen and experienced large birds, with enormous wingspans and golden feathers; others have felt, perceived, or received images of star beings that don't look human and look more like what we might call aliens; some see white-light beings, operating from the far reaches of space; others connect with tribes of magical women.

It's common to become aware of other planets or planes of existence: some talk about a crystal planet with an enormous crystal castle while others offer accounts of hovering in the darkness of space with beams of starlight around them while communing with otherworldly beings. Many have experienced conversations or communing with "the Council," a group of beings that offer high-level guidance and profound spiritual direction.

This list of examples could go on and on—that's the wondrous beauty of our Spirit Guides!

Often, when your high-level Spirit Guides connect with you, their messages feel weighty and carry a gravity or seriousness. Commonly, their guidance is delivered in short sentences or phrases, or as directives that are simultaneously intense and loving. They cut right to the core truth and never mince words. It often feels as if, suddenly and completely, the energy in the room entirely shifts, and there's a new sacredness in the air. These guides often communicate profound spiritual truths with a candor and a seeming simplicity.

There is a mystical, mysterious quality to these experiences. These guides and these experiences can be hard to wrap our human minds around. Of course, this is where mythology meets our reality, where we might pause and consider that these old cultural stories and traditions we've all heard about might just be rooted in humans' real experiences with the heavens. There is, after all, an undeniably long and in-depth recorded human history (from cave drawings and art to oral storytelling and written accounts) of mystical events, beings, and interactions occurring on our planet and with humans. Upon close examination, these stories and traditions all share central themes and consistency.

It seems we are decidedly linked to mystical beings and that the breadth of our existence expands well beyond our planet and our human consciousness.

You are guided and watched over. There is order in what seems to be chaos. Because your Soul is part and parcel of the Universe, you're connected to the mystical.

Just because it's perhaps challenging to make sense of this with the human mind doesn't mean these other worlds, dimensions, and beings don't exist. They are, in fact, very real...and your Soul knows it.

 ## SACRED INTENTION-SETTING:
Connecting with Your High-Level Spirit Guides

As we pause to open up and prepare to meet and get to know your high-level Spirit Guides, remember that this might feel different from working with your loved ones on the Other Side, or sitting next to your Soul Fire. Remember that this experience might feel more mystical, hard to describe, or otherworldly. Trust what comes to you.

When you're ready, read silently or aloud this intention:

I open to my high-level Spirit Guides. I welcome the experience of their presence and am curious about how this experience feels. I open to the mystical nature of my Spirit Guides and am curious about how they communicate. I welcome the guidance my high-level Spirit Guides have to give me and, upon receiving it, I bring it to my Soul Fire for safe keeping. I ask my Spirit Guides to stay in close contact with me and continue to offer me that which is in my Highest and Best Honor.

POWERING INTENTION WITH ACTION

Consider writing down, journaling, drawing, recording, creating art, or somehow making note of how this experience feels. Consider becoming more curious about the mystical nature of your Spirit Guides. Consider researching what you've seen or experienced, or looking for other cultures, myths, or stories that seem connected to your Spirit Guides. Consider returning to the Soul Fire to reflect and treasure the information you've collected.

Angels, Elementals, and Animal Souls

Rounding out your Spirit Team are a lovely variety of other spirits, guides, and Souls. These include angels, elementals (like fairies and nature spirits), and animal Souls. Of course, there are entire books written on these topics, detailing how these beings exist and operate. If any of these resonate with you, please pursue further reading and more in-depth exploration for yourself. *Surely, when something resonates with you and your curiosity is piqued, it's because you're meant to learn and know more.* Follow those intuitive breadcrumb trails—your Soul wants you to know more!

Here, we'll talk briefly about these beings.

ANGELS

Angels are beings that operate in their own realm. They are forces of light and goodness. Their specialty is love, light, strength, protection, nurturing, and divinely inspired guidance. Those who specialize in angel communication often say that we have angels assigned to us from birth.

Saint Jerome agrees: "How great the dignity of the soul, since each one has from his birth an angel commissioned to guard it."

Angels often feel loving and soft, understanding and nurturing, protective and strong. They respond to direct requests for assistance, protection, guidance, and clarity. If you feel that you need some nurturing and tenderness as you take a brave step forward, your angels are the ones to call on.

There's something pure and clear about the angelic realm, something straightforwardly and unconditionally loving. Don't hesitate to call on your guardian angels. Invite them in, welcome their presence and their gifts. Feel their nurturing, tender love like a soft blanket wrapped around you; allow their comfort to be with you as you bravely walk your path and build a life that's congruent with your Soul.

A Message from the Other Side

"You are not alone. Your angels—those who guard you with unconditional love and devotion—are of pure light and intention. They are always present, waiting, and ready to dispatch themselves on your behalf. All you need to do is ask. You are worthy of this request. You are worthy of their divine intercessions."

ELEMENTALS

If you're connected to the Elemental Realm, you'll know it! These beings are irreverent, clever, and fierce in their devotion. Guardians of and partners with nature, these beings, including fairies, gnomes, sprites, pixies, and others, are particularly fond of humans who love, revere, honor, and respect nature.

If you're meant to engage and interact with the Elementals, you likely will have known it from a young age. As a young child, you might have had a particular interest in fairies, building fairy houses in your backyard, or avidly reading books about fairies. Your children or the children in your life might carry these interests themselves, drawn to you because you understand this and will honor it.

You might feel elementals while walking in the woods, when you're working with animals, floating in the ocean, or sitting among the forest's trees. You might feel a presence walking along with you, or even a sense of watchful eyes upon you. Some people can see these little beings amongst the leaves, around the base of trees, or flitting around the water. More are able to capture Elementals in photographs; they usually appear as orbs or balls of colored light that can't be explained away as a trick of lighting or the camera lens.

Elementals have a decidedly fun, even mischievous, energy. They'll sometimes appear to "their people" as flashes of light, seen out of the corner of the eye. When you look more closely and directly, the light will be gone. Flashes of sudden, irreverent light are the calling cards of Elementals.

If the Elementals are part of your Spirit Team, it's likely you are profoundly and devoutly connected to nature.

Your path might include working with plant spirits, herbalism, healing through and with nature, water therapy, or working with flower essences. Any personal healing or restorative work you do, on behalf of your Soul, will be helped and advanced by your Elemental team. They are very keen on helping "their people" grow into the happiest, most vibrant versions of themselves.

These guides are loving and fun! If this discussion resonates with you, seek out resources and additional information, welcome spiritual experiences with nature, and open up to your Elemental guides. They offer irreverent reminders that your Soul is deeply connected to the Souls of plants, animals, trees, and all things in nature. This truth can be profoundly reassuring and comforting, especially as it offers a break from the intensity of the human world. Allow your Elemental guides to remind you, delight you, and call you further into communion with nature. Nature is where you'll find some of the deepest, most nourishing insights into your Soul.

ANIMAL SOULS

Animal Souls and Spirits are among the most loyal and steadfast of Spirit Guides. Animals often incarnate with us again and again throughout our lifetimes. It's not uncommon to find that your dog in your current lifetime was your horse in a previous lifetime and a cat in another lifetime.

As anyone who loves animals knows, they teach us about unconditional love. They are sweet little beacons of eternal love, kindness, tenderness, and friendship. They are forgiving and smart, intuitive and loyal, comforting and playful. Animal Souls offer us reminders that we are more than our human lives and experiences, that Souls forge deep and powerful bonds that transcend human experiences—and transcend species!

If one or more of your Animal Spirits is incarnated with you now, running around your house as your friendly dog or curled up in your lap as your loyal companion cat, embrace their Soul presence. Allow your animals to guide you, remind you, and teach you. Allow them to lead you to new places, physically and spiritually. Talk out loud to them, affirm with affection and confirm with presence that you hear them, receive them, and are grateful for them. Know that when you feel deep Soul connections with one or more animals, it's an indication that you and this Soul have been together before and are here, in this incarnation, together, for a reason.

Meanwhile, if the animals you love are on the Other Side, know that, just like your human loved ones who've crossed, these Souls are alive and well. Animals tend to cross more efficiently because they're not burdened with karma and the weight of life experiences that humans accumulate (and then need to sort through). Animal Souls often know when it's their time to cross and often do so with ease.

Because animals are so loyal and unconditionally loving, their Souls often station themselves right alongside you, journeying with you as you continue through your human lifetime. Sometimes they are able to reincarnate again and come back into your life as a different animal, some years later. Talk to them, embrace them, open to their presence in your life. It's very common to continue to feel your animals after they've crossed; some even say it's easier to feel animals than it is to feel human loved ones. This is because our bonds with our animals are closer to our spiritual nature: often telepathic, energetic, unspoken, and focused on our emotional and intuitive centers. It's more natural to relate to them as spirits.

Animal Spirits are unyieldingly loyal and often incarnate with us, over and over again, acting as transcendent touchstones over the course of many lifetimes.

If you have Animal Souls on your Spirit Team, they provide steady, unconditional love. They offer reminders that all is well and that we all return to Soul form, and that is inherently comforting. Animal Souls encourage you to continue your human journey, deepening your understanding of your spiritual nature and aligning with your Soul in faith, trust, and comfort. Animal Souls ask you to bravely heal your wounding and consider ways you might love yourself more wholly.

Finding Your Spirit Team

While your Spirit Team absolutely connects and sends messages within the context of your busy life, it's often powerful and useful to cultivate your own spaces of quiet and reflection. These more tranquil spaces grant you clear access to your guides, cutting through the noise and delivering insights, answers, and comfort in direct and immediate ways.

When you come to a place of openness, asking for the guidance and support you need, you are inherently poised to receive what is in your Highest and Best Honor.

For some, that's on the yoga mat or hiking up a mountain. For others, it's a daily walk or twenty minutes of meditation. For some, it's playing music or creating art. Sometimes, it's in quiet companionship with a human or animal friend. Other times, it's settling into silence in the car, bathtub, the woods, or bed.

Some find that a routine works best and that they look forward to their set-aside time to connect with their guides. Establishing a kind of sacred routine, perhaps a few times a week or even—hopefully—daily, to check in with your Spirit Team and yourself, creates a profoundly deep working relationship you'll surely come to count on over time. *The more often you connect with your Spirit Team, the deeper your relationship with them becomes.*

And, remember this: whether you create the space or not, your Spirit Team will find you! They will talk to you, show you, nag you, reveal to you, implore you—one way or another, they'll get your attention. Even if creating that space is challenging for you, know that your Spirit Team is always with you. They're yours, always. The key is for you to consciously value and decide that receiving their guidance is going to be an active part of your life, one step at a time.

 ## SACRED INTENTION-SETTING:
Creating Room for Your Spirit Team

It's valuable to, essentially, dust off a spot in your life for your Spirit Team. Find a place for them to sit and visit (so to speak) that works for you. Find this place where you're still or quiet or open to feel the sacred intimacy of this visit. You might return to your Soul Fire and invite them to join you there, or you might feel that you want to create a place of connection within your daily routine for them to join you. Please do what feels right for you, knowing you can shift, change, or grow this place of meeting at any time.

When you're ready, read silently or aloud this intention:

I welcome my Spirit Team into my life. I create space for them. I open channels of hearing, knowing, awareness, and receiving between my human self and my guides. I welcome my Spirit Team to join me here (in the place or space or time you've set aside) to share, communicate, illuminate, and commune. I affirm my willingness to meet my guides in this space and to seek their input with regularity. I will keep this space sacred and open; I will attend to it as an act of self-love and self-investment. I am worthy of this space and these meetings. I am worthy of the love and support my Spirit Team offers me.

 POWERING INTENTION WITH ACTION

Consider making a bit of a show of this exercise. Whether it's creating a space within your mind's eye or establishing a physical location or routine, consider doing so with strong commitment and intention. Consider saying to yourself, *"THIS is the space/place where I allow communion with my Spirit Team, and I will arrive here daily."* Create that new habit by returning to this space daily, decisively, and lovingly.

What Guidance Requires of You

As humans, we are conditioned and encouraged to look outside of ourselves for information, meaning, and validation. Many of our cultural structures, traditions, expectations, and systems teach us, from a young age, to look outside of ourselves to know ourselves. We are taught that someone who knows better than us must approve of or validate us. Our society rewards money, or at least the appearance of wealth. Many religious, political, governmental, educational, and familial systems demand that we obey authority figures and marginalize those with other viewpoints.

The result, often, of this kind of outside-of-us structure is that we feel disconnected, unworthy, less than, unlovable, or confused. Our sense of self suffers: What if you don't fit in? What if fitting in feels wrong and like a lie? What if seeking approval from outside authority figures sets you on a hamster wheel of seeking approval instead of understanding and developing who you truly are? What if aiming to be attractive, wealthy, successful, popular, well-liked, good, and approved of leads you further from your Soul instead of closer to it?

What if, instead of aligning with outside, arbitrary, humanly created societal norms, you are meant to seek and find the insights held within?

You are the center of your truth. You are meant to go out and gather perspective, insight, ideas, and experiences and then take them inward, weighing them against what you know, determining what feels right and true. You're meant to apply your inner compass, including your intuition, to help discern if what you've collected out there makes sense for you to take in, adopt, adapt, and integrate.

The development of this gateway is so important. Fundamentally important.

*You are not meant to blindly or fearfully take in what's presented to you by the outside world and allow it to identify or shape you without question or consideration. You are meant to interrupt this process and apply your internal filters, sense of self, knowledge, and awareness, and then take what fits, leave what doesn't, accept what you've learned about yourself, and **keep moving**. You are meant to define yourself.*

Discernment and Your Spirit Guides

Our Spirit Guides want you to take in their direction, guidance, advice, and input and use your discernment to determine how to move forward in a way that feels right and true. They will stretch you and challenge you and push you to move through fear. They will also offer understanding, compassion, and kindness when the leaps are significant, the path gets rocky, and the task of following what you know is true feels daunting.

Of course, all of this might just be a bit unnerving. It's one thing to consider the person you loved dearly and who treated you with tenderness is on the Other Side, gently guiding you from afar. That can be easier to take in, right? Sometimes, the notion of these high-level Spirit Guides and their mystical mysteriousness can be hard to fathom, unsettling, even scary.

It's not uncommon that people come face-to-face with a Spirit Guide in meditation and feel startled, or that a dream or a vision causes mind-bending anxiety. (*"What do you mean I was communing with star beings while hovering in the vastness of space?"*) Yes, this is big. Daunting. Hard to understand—even harder to explain. It's the stuff that's relegated to the movies, vilified in traditional society, and buried in the historical record. It takes courage and bravery to move past some of these doubts and fears and step into a place of welcoming connection to your Spirit Guides. It requires faith to remember and know that you yourself are mystical and spiritual and that this language is familiar.

And what about those difficult humans who cross over? How do we know if their Souls are friendly and showing up to help us? Yes, you're not meant to martyr them, but how do you separate your own feelings of hurt so that you don't miss an opportunity to heal?

*This is where **discernment** is essential. This is where you, as the seat of your own power and truth, are your greatest clarifying and stabilizing asset.*

Remember: you don't have to take in anything that doesn't resonate with you. Whether a societal rule, a familial mandate, or a message from your guides, you don't need to adopt anything as fact or truth in your life if it doesn't feel right to do so. You can choose what to engage with, and how far to take that engagement, each step of the way.

Also remember: fear, anxiety, nervousness, skepticism, and confusion aren't necessarily signs that you're confronting something that isn't right for you. Sometimes these reactions and emotions are invitations to look a bit deeper, gather more information, give something more space, or try a notion on for size. Sometimes, the discomfort is a sign that there's more for you to know, explore, and understand.

What's that line? And how will you know? How will you know what you should step into to explore further, despite discomfort? How will you know if something just isn't right for you? Discernment is how you'll know, and it comes with experience, practice, and engagement with your intuition and your Spirit Guides. It's a muscle you can develop because it's held deep within you.

Discernment is the cultivation of a practice of pausing and breathing, of checking in and determining, with your whole body, what resonates with you.

It's the practice of bringing divine guidance inside of you and feeling what belongs with you. Once there, nestled in your body, feel around. Use the power of intention to determine if what you're feeling is right and true, or, if parts of it are. Use the power of intention, perhaps with the *Highest and Best Honor* language, to declare that, if a piece of guidance isn't right for you to take in, you'll release it.

Discernment is about cultivating a practice of determining what feels right and true and then integrating that truth and guidance into your life. Discernment is an ability to trust yourself to notice what's coming from your outside world and decide which parts of it belong in your inner world. Discernment is knowing, believing in, and working with your sacred power of choice.

Remember that you have come here equipped with the tools you need, and discernment is among them. Discernment helps you determine what's right for you, at the right time, when to push a bit more, and when something isn't meant for you or in your *Highest and Best Honor*.

> *Discernment reminds you that you know the truth by the way it feels.*

SACRED INTENTION-SETTING:
Exploring Discernment

Let's return to your Soul Fire, sitting next to it with curiosity about where your power of discernment lives within you. Close your eyes and imagine yourself settling in next to your Soul Fire. Relax your body and allow the flames of your Soul Fire to warm and comfort you.

When you're ready, read silently or aloud this intention:

I welcome the awareness of my power of discernment. I look with curiosity for the seat of discernment within me and welcome deepening my relationship with it. I am open to receiving insight from my seat of discernment and receive, with curiosity, its messages, nudges, insights, guidance, and feedback. I notice what it feels like to receive information from my discernment. I notice what it feels like to have my discernment tell me that something is in my Highest and Best Honor. I notice what it feels like to have my discernment tell me that something is not in my Highest and Best Honor. I notice how I feel and know these truths within my body and my being. I commit to returning to this seat of discernment regularly, inquiring about what's best for me, and treating the guidance I receive as sacred and valuable for my Soul journey.

POWERING INTENTION WITH ACTION

Think of one lingering question, concern, or notion where you would like to have more clarity. Something that perhaps hasn't been clear to you. Something about which you're deeply curious. Hold that question close and settle into your seat of discernment and ask, remaining open and curious, if one answer or one direction is in your *Highest and Best Honor*. Practice using your discernment to gather insight about questions you have and steps you might take next on your journey.

Pairing Spirit Guidance with Action

Just as with intuition, the key to unlocking the power of spirit guidance is action.

Don't bargain with guidance (*"I'll believe if you show me this"* or *"I'll do what you ask if you give me that"*); instead, accept what's revealed and, as best you can, take an action step in that direction.

Your ability to honor truth and to be honest with yourself is directly related to how strong your intuition will become and how clear your ability to receive guidance will become. Intuition is like a muscle; the more you use it, the stronger and more defined it becomes. The same is true for spirit guidance; your relationship with it and its ability to positively impact your life will grow the more you trust it and use it.

You see, your Spirit Team wants to be helpful and useful to you; they want to help you heal, grow, and evolve. They want you to bravely face the stuff that keeps you fearful, limited, and small. That's the greatest gift you can give a loved one on the Other Side or your beloved Animal Spirit or any of those on your Spirit Team.

And, the wondrous thing is: when you pair this divine guidance with action, you build a direct, clear line to your Spirit Team and are much better able to receive and recognize their support, messages, and presence in your life.

Your Spirit Team wants to engage with you regularly, building a conversational relationship, just like your intuition.

Whether it's asking you to heal a childhood wound, clear some old karma, set healthy boundaries within complicated family systems, or honor a lifelong dream or goal, your guides ask you to return to yourself to clear the pathways to your Soul. Your Spirit Team knows firsthand the value of a human who has aligned with her Soul, and so, they prompt you to undertake the journey into the Soul, walking that pathway of self-love, divine connection, and self-compassion with bravery and courage.

A Message from the Other Side

"The greatest barriers humans have to receiving guidance are believing themselves unworthy or believing they know better. It takes simultaneous humility and courage to receive spirit guidance."

*"Awakening is not changing who you are,
but discarding who you are not."*

—Deepak Chopra

---

*"I can do nothing for you but work on myself...
you can do nothing for me but work on yourself!"*

—Ram Dass

Part Two

Living with the Soul

"What matters is how quickly you do what your soul directs."

—Rumi

———————————————————— ♥ ————————————————————

"You have to take risks. We will only understand the miracle of life fully when we allow the unexpected to happen."

—Paulo Coelho, *By the River Piedra I Sat Down And Wept*

A Grounded Journey

The path to the Soul requires action, and this need for experiential self-expression is one of the reasons why incarnating into human bodies offers us such value.

Being embodied in physical form lets us do what we need and long to do: experience and engage. We want to move, relate, feel, and act. We want to make choices and be self-directed. We, on a Soul level, crave complete immersion in the highs and lows of the physical experience. All of the energy generated around action and free will teaches us just how powerful we are—and our Souls like those kinds of lessons.

Our actions reveal to us who we are and prompt us to decide if we like what we see and, if not, to change course. Because our choices reveal the most profound truths about us, our lives are filled with moments of agency: decision points that present opportunities to grow, shift, refine, heal, decide, and define who and what we are.

Being human allows us to see, in living color, just who we are, as evidenced by our choices and actions. Being human also enables us to arrive, with deep conviction, at the awareness that, at any moment, we can choose who and what we are.

Action is a given. We're wired for it. Where it's derived from—a conscious, aware, healed place or a wounded, biased, unaware, unconscious place—is where we find the work of our lives.

When we commit to building lives in greater congruence with our Souls, we must have regard for the magnitude of our actions, choices, and free will. In accepting the truth about our innate power, the Soul then asks us to take responsibility for it. When you understand the awesome power within you to create your reality, it becomes fundamentally necessary that you use it wisely.

This pivot point is fundamental, sacred, and nonnegotiable. There is no spiritual journey without personal responsibility. There is no spiritual journey without a deep respect for the accountability we must have for ourselves, our choices, and what we carry within us, consciously and unconsciously.

There is a gravity in personal responsibility. Your Soul requires it. Taking responsibility for yourself, your choices, and everything you're consciously and unconsciously carrying within you can be deeply challenging. But it's not all hard work; just as with any sacred truth, there are glorious payoffs too. There is magnificent freedom and clarifying release in personal responsibility.

> *Deciding that you are ultimately accountable for who and what you are will change your life.*

The path to the Soul includes a series of preeminent universal truths and themes that, if embraced, offer opportunities to transform your life. Understanding and working with them—or, taking responsibility and mindful action—bring you to the crossroads of conscious choice and, ultimately, into alignment with your Soul.

Some of these universal truths and themes include:

- Accepting that you are here, in human form, in this incarnation, experiencing this lifetime, to be provoked and inspired to heal, evolve, learn, shift, and grow.

- Receiving and accepting the loving and divine assistance, tools, support, and guidance available to you on your journey.

- Taking responsibility for your role on the path to living in alignment with your Soul, stepping into full awareness that you are responsible for yourself and who you choose to be.

- Accepting that you are here to become more conscious and aware that your power of choice and your power of free will are creating, moment by moment, your experience. *In each moment, what you choose, consciously or unconsciously, is creating your human reality.*

- Accepting that what you choose can either help or hurt, further or hinder, create or destroy, uplift or confuse, advance or deter, be rooted in love or fear. Accepting that each choice you make can arise from *conscious intention,* originating from a place within that is aligned with your Soul.

- Accepting responsibility for this expansive power of choice, choosing to act with conscious intention, and, when you do not, pausing to realign, regroup, and adjust to make a more conscious choice. Pairing that responsibility with self-love, allowing yourself room to evolve and grow, forgiving yourself when necessary, and doing and being better when you know better.

- Receiving the gifts of personal responsibility: vibrancy, grounding, secure connections to your intuition and your Spirit Team, grace when you make mistakes and need to adjust, and a deep knowing that you're in control of yourself, no matter how chaotic your world feels.

You and your Soul are one, and your mission, should you choose to accept it, is to take responsibility for building a life that reflects that truth.

You are the one you've been waiting for. *You* are the one you've wanted to find. *You* are in charge of your life. You only need to accept that responsibility and then make a conscious commitment to living, one step at a time, from that awareness.

Finding, Cultivating, and Nourishing the Commitment to Live in Alignment with Your Soul

Let's begin by centering your awareness and coming to the grounded place of conscious living: the place where your commitment to your Soul resides.

Let's root and ground in this steadfast, fierce, motivated, optimistic, faithful, trusting, curious, responsible, empowered place.

Let's build an energetic space where your mindset shifts from one of fear to one of love—a place where your mindset shifts into a place of sacred personal power and deep knowing.

Here, you don't need to search for something intensely; instead, simply settle into this seat of commitment, this seat of personal power, this seat from which you are entirely able to live your life in congruence with your Soul.

With gentle curiosity, open to the possibility of releasing what needs to be released, of allowing what needs to be allowed, and of expanding what needs to be expanded.

This place is steadfast, eternal, and powerful while offering grace, invitation, and gentleness.

This place contains the deep knowledge that personal responsibility is one of the most transformational forces in the Universe. This place knows that one human, stepping into their personal responsibility, immediately emanates light and uplifts the Universe.

This place offers a constant reminder that one small choice, shift, or action has the power to transform your life.

Here, you know that these small, intentioned steps offer you access to the magnificent, loving, helpful energy provided by the Universe.

Here, you know that building alignment with your Soul comes with one intentioned step at a time. Here, you know that your power lies within you and within your choice to step forward.

In this place, we'll build, cultivate, and nourish your commitment to your Soul and your commitment to your most whole, vibrant self.

This is the place where divine forces and your power of choice converge. This is the place where you know, deeply and sincerely, that you can do anything, that your life is yours to create, and that there is freedom in walking the path to the Soul.

Rooted in this powerful place, you can commit to doing the very best you can in each moment. And, when you have not, this is the place where you find grace, self-compassion, and the freedom to realign and adjust.

This place offers you motivation, forgiveness, reassurance, and inspiration. This place is your source of action, choice, and power. This is the place of inspired and intentioned action.

This place of commitment never wavers or judges; it offers you, always, a chance to begin again, try once more, or do or be better.

This place is where the divine and universal forces swirling around you do their very best work and offer you their sacred partnership.

 ## SACRED INTENTION-SETTING:

A Ceremony of Sacred Responsibility and Commitment

Spend some time considering how these notions of personal responsibility, the powers of choice and free will, and committing to these, feel to you. You might feel some resistance or pressure; you might feel unsure or nervous; you might be afraid to fail. You might also feel twinges of excitement or empowered readiness; you might feel an ah-ha moment brewing or even relief. Welcome what comes up without judgment. Be kind to yourself and embrace where you are, right now, in this process. Remember: if something uncomfortable, daunting, confusing, or challenging arises, respond with self-compassion and allowance. There is no need to solve any troubling feelings right now; rather, accept what appears and meet it with a sense of willingness and compassionate responsibility. Remember: taking responsibility is taking care of yourself. It's an act of self-care and a gesture of self-love.

When you're ready, read silently or aloud this intention:

I allow connection with my Soul.

I allow my commitment to living in alignment with my Soul to inspire me, to direct me, to nudge me, to inform me.

I embrace personal responsibility and the gifts it has to offer me.

I embrace a sacred commitment to more deeply know and understand my part in my life and on my path to my Soul.

I allow myself to receive intuitive guidance and helpful notes from my Spirit Guides.

I allow myself to know that I am worthy.

I allow myself to receive what is in my Highest and Best Honor, even when I doubt my worthiness.

I allow curiosity about the next step on the journey toward my Soul.

I allow myself the time and space to honor, understand, heal, and consider the messages my Soul has for me.

I allow unconditional love.

POWERING INTENTION
WITH ACTION

Consider what has come up for you in reading and processing these ideas of personal responsibility, choice, and free will. What has your relationship with personal responsibility looked like in the past? Does this concept of taking responsibility as a means to step into your personal power resonate with you? Consider writing or journaling, creating some art, or engaging in something creative to honor and work with what has come up for you. Consider that you do not, at this time, need answers or problem-solving; instead, be open and curious about how you might further engage with this notion of personal responsibility.

"When we strive to become better than we are,
everything around us becomes better, too."

—Paulo Coelho, *The Alchemist*

———————————————— ♥ ————————————————

"You either walk inside your story and own it, or you stand
outside your story and hustle for your worthiness."

—Brené Brown

Chapter Four

With Great Power Comes Great (Personal) Responsibility

When you take responsibility for yourself and your journey, you immediately connect to the source of your personal power. In stepping into responsibility and, therefore, your power, you'll discover new ways to understand yourself and your life experiences. Here, you'll find that confusion calms, and pain eases. Here, your emotions no longer identify you, they inform you. Here, you discover that accepting responsibility instantly amplifies your intuition, and spirit guidance feels closer and becomes more evident.

Accepting personal responsibility changes you instantly and places you in the driver's seat of your life. There isn't anything you cannot accomplish on behalf of yourself and your path from this place of conscious awareness, willingness, and empowerment.

Personal responsibility is fundamental to your human experience and your Soul journey. It's what can make the most confusing, challenging, emotional, and wounding of human experiences something you can work with—something that, if you allow it, evolves you. Yes, there will be work to do, but the act of accepting personal responsibility immediately and instantaneously creates an alchemical, even mystical, transformation that is comforting, reinforcing, and illuminating.

Everything in your life is a reflection of your relationship with your Soul. Your Soul wants you to shift, change, grow, question, wonder, consider, press on, try, adjust, and rework. It's always offering you an invitation to connect. This invitation is an ever-present gentle—though persistent—call to discover how you might deepen your relationship with your Soul, by clearing, healing, and restoring the pathways to it. The connection between that gentle, persistent force and you is your human experience.

What you're experiencing as a human being is gently and persistently endeavoring to show you where you need to heal, become more aware or conscious, and deepen alignment with your Soul.

The ultimate question is: Will you take responsibility for exploring what this persistent force is showing you?

Your power to transform your life lies in your answer to that sacred question.

Your Human Experience Is a Compass

You've come to Earth equipped with an inner compass, and that compass's true north is calibrated to your Soul. The events and experiences of your life—relationships, internal monologues, work, hobbies, habits, conflicts, drama, choices, places of fulfillment, peace, joy, troubles, confusion, longings, and questioning—act as readings on that compass, drawing you closer to your magnetic truth.

This compass, powered by your human experiences, leads you down the path of self-exploration. Along the way, your human experiences show you where and what to heal, nurture, amplify, and restore. These experiences reveal what you're carrying and offer opportunities to release, repair, or transcend what binds you.

In building alignment with your Soul, you will be asked to accept responsibility for healing whatever keeps you from it. You'll find the pathways to your Soul that have become confused or obstructed by the human experience and be urged to take a look at the hard stuff that lives there. You'll then be asked to restore those pathways, healing yourself, and transcending your human experience as you do so. You'll find, as you move along this journey, that you're less bogged down by what happens in your life and more likely to remember that you're having a spiritual experience designed to evolve you. You'll find that your human experiences don't stick to you—they'll inform you.

The Soul journey, guided by what you're experiencing, will ask you to tend to what in you needs love, nurturing, care, and restoration. It will also ask you to notice and build upon what brings you joy, fulfillment, contentment, vibrancy, and connection—those moments where you, in your human form, *feel your Soul*. The journey to the Soul will demand you do these things on behalf of yourself, as courageous acts of self-love, self-compassion, and sacred responsibility.

The Soul journey asks you to tend to yourself with conviction so that you become more whole and purely rooted in your spiritual essence. When you love yourself enough to heal yourself, you embody the unconditional love the Universe offers and become a beacon of that universal force.

Understanding the concept that what happens in your life shows you the way to your Soul is the key to moving beyond the limits of the human experience. Understanding how to make this concept practical, accessible, and workable is the key to making your human life an extension of your Soul.

Finding and Building Points of Joyful Alignment

It's always a good idea to start with what you know, or, at least, with what's immediately accessible. Your Soul wants you to succeed! So, let's begin with some "easy" wins.

Imagine joy.

Imagine irreverence.

Imagine laughing hysterically, tears in your eyes, with abandon.

Imagine a moment when you felt fulfilled, content, vibrant, *alive*.

Call up a moment where you felt connected to something more substantial, even whole. Remember how your body felt, the smile on your face, the weightlessness. Remember that thrilling accomplishment: at work, at school, on stage, in your creative process, within a relationship. Remember feeling proud of yourself, on top of the world, on fire. Remember moments of feeling completely connected to your child, your friend, your love, yourself; recall the wholeness of that connection and the delight that kind of love and congruence brought you.

Imagine seizing a single moment and collecting it, placing it alongside other such moments, like a string of bright lights. *"I want more of these in my life,"* you say. *"I want to feel more of this."*

We often talk of what isn't right or what's broken and needs healing or betterment. But don't forget: *there is so much that is just right.*

There is so much that is pristinely good, right, pure, loving, sacred, fulfilling, inspirational, and alive. There is always light, all around us. You can always choose these things for yourself. Remember this. Know this.

Living in alignment with your Soul is to notice these moments of fullness and vibrancy and to *consciously choose to create more of them.*

A human life aligned with your Soul asks you to remember moments of fulfilled rightness and never to lose sight of the hope, inspiration, and invitation they carry. These moments are indeed brilliant little lights—and you can have as many of them as you want. You can have a whole life filled with these dazzling lights!

Your divine birthright is to build a life glowing with your Soul's brightness. As the director of that process, you decide what comes in, what goes out, and what you do or do not make room for.

Just as this journey inspires you to draw fulfilled moments toward you and create more opportunities in your life for these kinds of moments to arrive and thrive, it also includes bravely acknowledging what does not belong or feel right, and releasing it.

Practically, this kind of existence includes making bolder choices, based upon truths that you feel, deeply, within your being. These decisions or changes require bravery and courage. They'll challenge you. They'll stretch you. But, also, they'll enrich your life. From changing your job or ending a relationship to starting your own business or shifting your schedule to make room in your week to create art, this way of life asks you to tell yourself the truth and then to accept responsibility for acting on that truth.

Releasing what distracts from or occupies space that could otherwise be filled with more truthful, soulful experiences is fundamental. You might find yourself turning off the television, limiting social media, or reducing your social commitments in favor of heading into nature to sit and ponder, taking a self-help workshop, or consciously engaging in quiet, centering activities. When you reduce the energetic clutter and distracting noise of life, opting instead for what nourishes and refuels you, you're operating in alignment with your Soul.

Here, intuition strengthens, and Spirit Guides arrive because you've made room for your Soul. Here, you'll discover that removing what distracts and depletes grants you unfiltered access to what heals and nourishes.

It takes conscious awareness to notice light-filled moments of joy and the moments that nourish your Soul Fire. It then takes conscious choice and action to create more of these moments and to remove what distracts from them. The beauty is that these are the spots where you can make decisive changes and nearly instant progress—*and it feels so good*. Making changes and embracing the important victories that come from them will help build momentum.

That momentum will help you continue making the right kinds of changes and shifts, building stamina, know-how, and self-trust for the times when the work feels harder and is less immediately rewarding.

SACRED INTENTION-SETTING:
Connecting to Moments of Joy

Our Souls want us to remember and connect with what brings us joy, fulfillment, and vibrancy. These are the places where we, as humans, truly experience the essence of our Souls. These moments are where we align with what's possible and remember that hope and faith are life-giving forces. Therefore, it's immeasurably valuable to note, honor, and harness these moments—and the energies contained within them—so that you create an indelible imprint you can perpetually reference.

When you're ready, read silently or aloud this intention:

I open with joyful curiosity to the vibrant essence of my Soul. I welcome the moments of joy, vibrance, happiness, irreverence, connection, and light in my life. I appreciate the opportunity to re-experience these moments right now.

As I do this, I notice how these experiences enter and fill my body: I feel them fill my heart, stabilize my core, ease my mind, and bring peace to my body. As I feel these experiences and their energies, I invite more of these into my life. I welcome into my life more moments of natural joy, uplifting vibrancy, and life-affirming connection.

I remind my mind, my heart, my body, and my Soul that these moments are fully available to me and that I am intrinsically worthy of them. I remind myself that I have the power to find, seek, choose, and draw in these moments as I journey through my day. I remind myself that I can remove or release what does not bring me joy or stands in the way of it.

POWERING INTENTION
WITH ACTION

Consider how you might memorialize this experience. You could draw a picture of what you experienced or of these energies. You might choose to journal about these moments, listing them and amplifying them with your own words or doodles. You might choose one experience in particular and write a reminder word or phrase on a Post-it Note and hang it on your mirror or place it in your planner to remind you of its magnificent power. Or, you might make an *"I want more of THIS!"* list and interact with it daily, centering your attention and power of intention each time you see it. Consider how you might prompt yourself to *feel* this joyful energy regularly.

A Courageous Deep Dive

For each of us, there is some measure of in-depth exploration and profound healing on the Soul journey. Just as there are light, joyous, and vibrant spaces for all of us, there are less clear spaces asking for our exploration, attention, and understanding.

These spaces might hold confusion or trauma; we might know full well what's there or, we might not. These places are where the human journey has gotten hard, heavy, depleting, devastating, exhausting, and we've fallen out of alignment with our Souls. These are spaces that create painful, challenging, and exhausting patterns in our lives and, if ignored, numbed, suppressed, or denied, cost us our wholeness and vibrancy.

What has happened to create these spaces within you is not your fault; your power lies, however, in knowing that you can face what's occurred, what's impacted you, and *choose* to heal.

You can take your power back from what's happened to you by taking responsibility for your own healing.

Healing is a journey and a process. It isn't one session with a provider or a single workshop or a quick read in a book. These things may be catalysts for the healing process, but rarely create the healing itself. Healing is a commitment to get to know yourself more thoroughly and, especially, those spaces within you that feel much more convenient to ignore.

Healing is gathering the courage to take a deep dive into yourself, facing what you find with bravery, and carrying the knowledge that you can transform what you find.

Healing is using your powers of responsibility and choice to become more aware of who you are and what you're putting out into the world. Healing is embracing your capacity to change and refine yourself, striding decisively toward a life that reflects your true spiritual nature.

What's Unconscious in You Is Playing Out Around You

An essential truth powering this process of self-awareness and healing is this: anything that is unconscious within you is asserting great force, even control, over you and your life.

What you are not aware of, consciously, remains an energetic force within you that will play out in your life, until you notice it and take responsibility for it.

The difficult, wounding, and traumatic events of your life are contained within you. The physical, emotional, psychological, and energetic components of these experiences sit within the human body, not as a punishment or to make you suffer, but so you'll come face-to-face with what has occurred and, ideally, choose to heal yourself. These experiential imprints remain until you're ready to look at them and, ultimately, transcend them.

When we lack the tools, strategies, support systems, or willingness to look at and deal with what's contained within us, our experiences lodge within our bodies. The traumas that remain buried, unaddressed, unhealed, unhonored—unconscious—seep into our waking human life, creating circumstances and patterns that reflect their presence.

The patterns in our lives are reflective of experiences, narratives, beliefs, or unawareness embedded in our unconscious selves. Patterns will continue until we pause and ask: *"What is the lesson here for me? What am I meant to notice? What am I meant to discover about myself? How can I step into greater self-awareness and take responsibility for what this pattern is telling me? What needs to change so that I am healthier, more empowered, or living my truth?"*

When you're feeling overwhelmed by or powerless against the patterns in your life—when you're suffering—this is an invitation to look more closely and remember that you are in control of your life. You have the power, at any moment, to say, *"Enough. I am ready to live differently."*

Let's work with an example to illustrate these concepts.

Imagine you grew up in a home where there wasn't enough. Perhaps a parent was chronically jobless, experiencing a disability, or struggling with addiction, and as a result, there was never enough money. From electricity and heat to food and clothing, your basic needs weren't consistently met, and as a child, you learned that you could never predict when there wouldn't be enough. Day to day, week to week, you weren't sure what to expect and became anxious and fearful.

This is trauma. Even if your parent was lovely and well-meaning, the experience of not having basic needs met registers in your body as a trauma. This experience—and the breadth of its emotional and psychological content—is contained within your body. You're human; you don't have a choice. It's there.

What you do have a choice about is how aware you are of its presence.

The measure of how this childhood experience will impact you is determined by how consciously you honor it, healing what comes up, and being compassionate to yourself when it does.

Our paths are not linear, so an experience or theme from childhood will come up on and off over time, depending on how aware we are of it as a force in our lives.

And so, if this was your childhood experience, the themes of lack and scarcity, fear and anxiety, likely play out in adulthood. You might find yourself struggling to maintain a job or manage money well. Or, you might find yourself living the other extreme: focused intensely on making money and finding that, no matter how much you make, it never feels like it's enough. You might work so obsessively that you sacrifice your marriage, children, and other areas of your life. Or, you might find that you are attracted to people like your struggling parent, building relationships with people who are unable to provide stability in their own lives, and so you strive to do it for them.

More subtly, you might feel a nagging emptiness in your life. You might find that no amount of stability in the form of work, money, relationship, shelter, food, or the trappings of human "safety" fills the void. You're safe and have, by all accounts, risen above where you came from, but you remain sad, anxious, fearful, or depressed.

As you move through life, whatever portions of this wounding remain unhealed and lodged within you, will play out, creating patterns of behavior and experience in your human life designed to get you to become conscious of what's been just below the surface.

You see, the patterns will release when you find the lesson. The replay will stop when you become conscious of what's driving it. This wounding doesn't want you to suffer; it wants you to awaken to it and heal.

You might ask why your Soul would agree to all of this. Why this fear and suffering? What an elaborate show of difficulty, right? Well, in this case, let's consider what profound lessons are offered. Imagine taking a deep dive into this wound and its healing; imagine what you might find there.

In honoring how afraid you were as a child, you could discover, as an adult, that you have a steady power to make good, prudent choices in your life, creating stability and safety. In understanding the depths of the anxiety this situation creates, you might discover the sacred power of meditation as a means to bring mindfulness and peace into your body.

A deep dive into this wound might show you that true happiness comes from wise balance, not from a workaholic franticness. You might discover that, in transcending this childhood experience, your calling is a career in empowering others, teaching adults to read, working with underprivileged children as a tutor, or fundraising for the homeless. In honoring the frightened, needy child you were, you might discover a new love for yourself and find that love transforms the way you treat yourself and others.

Our experiences, especially the difficult ones, influence us. When we choose to be conscious of those experiences and allow them to inform and inspire us, sacred opportunities arise to transcend our human experience and align with our Soul. From stopping the unhealthy cycle of the workaholic lifestyle to changing the pattern of taking on and enabling others, from honoring deeply held anxiety with compassion and self-love to allowing a painful childhood experience to create healthy inspiration in your life, these conscious responses to your pain are magnificently powerful. These conscious responses enable you to honor, heal, transform, and transcend what happened in your childhood. These conscious responses allow you to take control of your life and decide who you want to be.

> *"Let difficulty transform you. And it will. In my experience, we just need help in learning how not to run away."*
>
> —Pema Chodren

You have the power to change anything—anything—about yourself. You can declare that a pattern in your life has exhausted, depleted, hurt, disempowered, or de-valued you for long enough and that *this* is the moment where you begin anew.

Notice the patterns in your life. They reveal what's buried within you. Notice where you're out of balance, in pain, or feeling powerless. These are the places of invitation for self-exploration, healing, and conscious awareness. These are the places within you that want to know your Soul.

 ## SACRED INTENTION-SETTING:
Discovering a Pattern and the Truth It Holds

What we've discussed here is, undoubtedly, big. As such, you're encouraged in this exercise to work with something that feels appropriate for you at this time. Please do not think that you need to go digging for some massive piece of truth if you're not quite ready; instead, open up to what feels right for you, at this time, at this moment. Remember you can always return to this intention, choosing to go deeper and deeper. There is never a rush to some kind of finish line, nor is there an urging to take up something that is before its time. Trust what comes up and welcome what's ready for you right now.

When you're ready, read silently or aloud this intention:

I open up with curiosity to a pattern in my life that is costing me my essence. I open up with curiosity to a pattern that is depleting, disempowering, or holding me back. With compassion, I look at this pattern as it's presented to me, noting how often this pattern has come up in my life and for how long.

I notice commonalities in my life experiences or relationships wherein this pattern was present. I see commonalities in how I felt in those experiences or relationships and particularly, what this pattern cost me at those times.

I consider whether I am ready to commit to becoming more consciously aware of this pattern in my life. I consider what I might restore in my life or gain if I become more aware of this pattern. I consider what might release or end if I become more aware of this pattern. I consider committing to allowing this pattern to become conscious one safe step at a time, so that I may notice it, acknowledge it, and then choose something that better honors me.

POWERING INTENTION WITH ACTION

Note the pattern that came up for you. Note that, likely, it's a bit of a complicated story. It likely runs deep and goes back a long time. It probably has wound in and out of your life for some time. Remember that it's brave to look at your patterns and courageous to bring them to the conscious forefront so that you can choose to disassemble them in favor of healthier, more conscious choices. If you're ready to commit to doing this, consider what feels best for you. Do you need some additional support in the form of a coach, energy worker, or therapist? Do you feel invigorated and ready to begin shifting this old, previously subconscious belief or wound? If so, what's the next right step in doing so? Please take this at a pace that feels right and true. And remember: you can always try, pause, reconsider, and try again. The Soul never demands a rush; it simply asks you to begin. Take good care of yourself.

Personal Responsibility:
A Gift to Yourself and the World

Your duty, to yourself and the world around you, is to find the unconscious places within you and choose to take responsibility for them. Whatever is unhealed in you is being projected out into the world; whatever is unconscious in you is playing out as theater around you. It's all so you'll notice and hopefully, so you'll say, *"Ah, that's mine, let me take that in and go work with it. Let me take responsibility for that and go see about it."*

A constant in the experience of life is the law of karma. As a Universal force of balance, karma is about developing compassion, empathy, personal responsibility, and a strong Soul alignment that purifies your presence in the world.

Because what we hold subconsciously is projecting itself outside of us, we're at risk of sending our wounds out into the world if we aren't taking responsibility for them.

Karma wants to teach us to take responsibility for ourselves and what we do, and be accountable for how we impact who and what is outside of us. When we clean up our inner worlds and, therefore, what we're contributing to the world around us, we can be powerful forces of love and light.

This isn't always so easy. It takes bravery, and a willingness to challenge ourselves and release what often feels comfortable.

You see, we live in a humanly created society where it's very—very—easy to believe that our humanness is the extent of us, especially the shortcomings and flawed parts of our humanness. We live in a society that thrives on us forgetting our power and shirking personal responsibility.

In our society, we are fed messages that reinforce the illusion of our humanness. We are evaluated by and reduced to how we look, the clothes we wear, or what we weigh. Money, power, and material assets are barometers of success, happiness, and wholeness. We are divided by race, class, gender, sexual orientation, nationality, and political party—and then encouraged to distrust, blame, scapegoat, and hate whoever is "other."

These curated messages from corporations, government, and wealthy powers that be are fed to us via television, news, and social media. They're designed to keep us fearful, believing there is never enough of anything, and inclined to hand over our personal power in exchange for a false sense of safety, protection, or belonging.

It takes great awareness not to be swallowed whole. It takes conscious observation, commitment, and choice to disconnect your sense of self from these messages that reinforce the false illusion that you are a limited, weak, flawed, shallow human being separate from an undying spiritual center.

Incarnating as a human being comes with the weighty responsibility of not forgetting that you're a Soul amidst a popular culture that thrives on you forgetting your Soul and losing yourself to your human experience.

You aren't meant to languish here, stuck, or to suffer in old wounds, trauma, and narratives. You aren't meant to lose yourself to the assertions of a power-hungry, top-down hierarchical society. You are meant to notice what's happening in your world and say, *"Enough! What is this showing me about where I need to honor, care for, heal, and love myself? And how soon can I begin to do it?"*

You are here to remember your Soul and to engage in the transformational act of becoming responsible for your human self. You are meant to come to know, firmly, that you are the seat of your own power and to build a life that's inspired by and reflective of your spiritual center.

A Message from the Other Side

"Your duty is to learn about your own power and to reckon with the patterns and choices that cause you to deny your own power. Your duty is to come to understand how powerful you are and, therefore, how responsible you must be. Your duty is to come to know and love yourself so resolutely that compassionate awareness and kind love are what you offer the world. You are co-creating reality on the Earth."

The Forces of Love and Fear

Love and fear, say many spiritual teachers and gurus, are the only two forces in the Universe.

That resonates, doesn't it?

What makes these forces active and dominant in our human lives is our level of personal responsibility. When we aren't taking responsibility for ourselves, we're more susceptible to fear, and therefore, we draw to us the things that match that vibration—that energetic signature.

When we are dominated by fear, we trust ourselves less, experience more confusion, and cling to excuses to avoid change or necessary leaps. When we're fearful, we doubt our intuition and our guides, and we are more likely to feel alone.

When we operate with personal responsibility, we are more inclined to be working with the powerful force of love.

Taking responsibility for yourself and your life will, almost always, turn fear on its head and draw you, naturally, into the magnificent power of love.

If personal responsibility requires fierce commitment, then love is the sweet and nourishing other side of that coin.

Your Soul Counted on Your Experiences

When your Soul readied for this incarnation, it established what it wanted to learn. That is, before you arrived here, in this lifetime, in human form, your Soul essentially sketched out what it wanted to experience, understand, learn, engage with, heal, and evolve through.

While our Souls set intentions and goals, there isn't one specific destined path; instead, there are countless ways our Souls can learn lessons and experience conscious evolution. Between the hallmarks of the human experience (our relationships, jobs, children, families, conditioning, emotions, awakenings, growth, pain, etc.) and the perpetual influence of spiritual dynamics (Universal truths and laws, intuition, Spirit Guides and guidance, past lifetimes, awakenings, mystical interventions, etc.), life lessons are always teed up for your consideration. Add to that your free will and power of choice, and you have an infinite number of combinations of experiences and options before you.

Fortunately, all of those possibilities share a compelling common intention: to wake you up.

You see, your Soul has sacred goals and intentions, great themes, and powerful dynamics it wants to explore, understand, work on, and even transcend.

Your Soul signed on for all of this because it was ready to powerfully evolve thanks to the intensity of the human experience.

You're here to allow yourself to be changed, by healing what wounds you and returning to spiritual truth.

Suffering presents perennial opportunities to rise and find the greatest version of you. It's up to you to determine how directly you do so.

When you embrace the Soul journey and regard your life experiences as invitations to learn more about yourself, clear blocks, gain understanding, and awaken, you're engaging directly and efficiently with your Soul's goals and intentions.

Your Soul counted on this—even the hard stuff (*especially* the hard stuff!)—as a mechanism for awakening.

Your Soul has already determined your success.

This is why the healing journey is so extraordinary; if you choose it, if you take responsibility for your part in walking it, it'll bring you right back to your Soul, to your nourishing center.

SACRED INTENTION-SETTING:
Checking In with Your Soul

Let's pause here to consider this truth: your Soul knows why you're here, what you're working on, and what you're ready to transform. Let's return to your Soul Fire, consult with it, and ask it: *What does my Soul want me to know or notice about my life experiences?*

When you're ready, read silently or aloud this intention:

I imagine returning to my Soul Fire. I sit down next to it, feeling its warmth and nourishing energy. As I sit next to my Soul Fire, I allow my body to fully relax, releasing any tension I am holding, and fully accepting restful support.

I open with curiosity and love, asking: What does my Soul want to tell me about my life experiences? What am I meant to notice about my life experiences? How have my life experiences contributed to my evolution, growth, and transformation? How have my life experiences illuminated my life's path? How has my Soul communicated with me through my life experiences? What might I now notice that I didn't before? How might I go deeper into my Soul connection and find a greater understanding of the insights my life experiences are offering me?

POWERING INTENTION WITH ACTION

It's powerful and comforting to remember that your Soul is entirely loving and supporting, always guiding and empowering you. Love yourself by reducing the clutter and noise in your life so that you can more clearly connect and listen. Where is there distraction, emotional clutter, or unhealthy noise in your life that takes you away from connection with your Soul? How might you reduce those intrusions and instead prioritize quiet time with your Soul, receiving, listening, and just being? What could you do today to reduce the noise? What could you release? What nourishing routine or habit could you begin?

Personal Responsibility Is the Key to Changing Your Life

In walking courageously along these Soul pathways, we find truths and insights that have been there all along. When we acknowledge what we find there, these reminders promote powerful change in our lives.

We so often ignore, deny, numb, or push away these reminders of truth. They're inconvenient; we are afraid of change. We become paralyzed with worry that what's on the other side of change is less stable or safe than where we are now. We struggle to release the comfort of our suffering, sometimes preferring to be victims of life or our parents or our childhood. It's comfortable to be the victim; we might get a lot of attention from that role, and it often protects us from having to take responsibility and make actual change.

Whatever about our suffering we've aligned with—perhaps as the victim or as the wounded child or the warrior who doesn't have time for emotion—we have to be prepared to release.

Healing means knowing that, in our human resilience, we have in some way, come to identify with our wounds, pain, or suffering, and letting go of that identification is necessary.

Be brave and courageous in telling yourself the truth about who you are, what you're feeling, and what needs your attention. Be bold in your willingness to release the parts of your story or your pain that you've adopted as badges of honor or identity that no longer serve you or are holding you back.

Making It Practical

When we act responsibly, staying in touch with our experiences and emotions so that they don't unconsciously become projected out into the world around us, we stand firmly in our power. And it takes a lot of courage to stand here. For most of us, we become aware that something within us needs attention when we feel it. It takes awareness, practice, and courage to stand right here: where it's painful, raw, guilt-ridden, angry, scary, confusing, and daunting.

You see, you cannot heal what you don't feel. You cannot change anything when you aren't conscious of it. You cannot shift or shed anything that you're bypassing, stuffing, or projecting out at someone else. Your power is in feeling, in telling yourself the truth about what you're feeling, and in your choice to be responsible for what you're feeling by examining and endeavoring to understand it.

Valuing personal responsibility enough to adopt it as a lifelong personal practice is one of the great secrets to life.

To make it practical, we need to initiate and maintain the habit of pausing, noticing, and self-inquiry. We need to develop our own personal practice of emotional welcoming and self-reflection.

Let's break it down.

ALLOW EMOTION TO INFORM YOU

Making personal responsibility a practical and workable theme in your life requires getting comfortable with your emotions and committing to stopping any patterns or habits you have around blocking what you feel.

Allow your emotions to travel through your body, noticing them and welcoming them as helpful messengers from your inner world.

We're so used to issuing quick—and unconscious—reactions to what we feel and then redirecting that emotion. So much of this happens without us even noticing it. Therefore, it might feel strange, daunting, or even unsettling simply to *allow* emotion, but that doesn't mean you are not capable of doing it.

For many of us, it's a foreign process; your body might react with nausea or panic or anxiety, you might experience physical tension or dizziness, or you might feel fearful that allowing your emotions will cause them to spiral out of control.

As you shift into emotional awareness, and away from ignoring or suppressing or being taken away with your emotions, there will be a period of getting used to this new normal. Breathe, talk to trusted loved ones, give yourself space or quiet time; take care of yourself in this process of allowing, feeling, and observation. Remember: your emotions don't own you or govern you, instead, they are dutiful and loving messengers from your body and your Soul about what in you needs your attention.

NOTICE WITHOUT JUDGMENT

Be aware of the way your body reacts and any physical sensations that accompany your emotions and feelings. Notice the way your mind reacts, especially the narratives that come up (*"I'm not safe," "This is just like when I was a kid and 'xyz' happened," "I'm not good enough," "I have to work harder," "No matter what I do, I never get ahead," "I'm never going to find someone who loves me for me."*)

Being aware—noticing—will take practice, too. And acceptance. We're accustomed to being almost preemptive in our snap judgments about ourselves and what we're experiencing. So often, we aren't even conscious of the ways emotional content triggers reactions, assumptions, conditioning, narratives, blame, defensiveness, and powerlessness.

The practice of noticing without judgment gives you the opportunity to stop these old loops in their tracks.

When these narratives are buried subconsciously, they run rampant without your awareness and have free rein over you. If you're able to pause, feel, and catch what's coming up, you're at the mighty and sacred precipice of being *informed* by your emotional responses. Here, your emotions are the messengers they're meant to be—and you're the conscious, self-aware person you're meant to be.

Don't hesitate to spend some time in this portion of the process. Frankly, you can't practice this enough! Practice noticing your reactions, the rise of emotion in your body, the thoughts that are almost automatically triggered, the way those thoughts impact you, and how you feel—about yourself, other people, or your situation. Practice breathing through this process, reminding yourself that you aren't defined by what's processing through you.

It won't take long before this process doesn't feel so foreign or new. Sooner than you might expect, you'll experience the empowerment, relief, and safety that comes with noticing what comes up within you. You'll undoubt-edly feel more in control in your life, and you'll develop a new sense of self-trust and self-awareness.

MOVE INTO CURIOUS AND GENTLE INQUIRY

As you get more comfortable with noticing what's com-ing from within, step into self-inquiry. As you develop the ability to stop and notice your emotions, you can begin to ask gentle and curious questions about what's happening.

- What emotions are coming up for me?

- What messages do these emotions carry with them?

- What am I meant to see or observe?

- Do I recognize this emotion and what it's carrying? Does this remind me of a pattern in my life?

- What do I need to take responsibility for in this partic-ular situation?

- What is mine? What isn't mine?

- What old narrative arises within this experience? When in my life did that narrative take root? Is it true?

- Is this something I feel often? When do I typically encounter this feeling?

- Is this feeling or thought fear-based? Is it rooted in reality?

- How do I feel about myself in this experience? What narratives or self-talk come up within this experience? Are those narratives true? Is that self-talk accurate?

- Is this something I want more or less of in my life?

You may ask some or all of these questions or you may come up with a list of your own. Lean into this practice of self-inquiry and feel, watch, and experience that you have the power to stop "automatic" responses and take control of your own emotional and experiential process.

> *Self-inquiry will teach you—and prove to you—that you are not powerless in chaotic human moments. It will show you how to work with your Soul in the throes of your human experience.*

The process of gentle inquiry is the key to transforming what previously ran rampant in your body and mind into informative and insightful direction.

CONSIDER A MORE CONSCIOUS CHOICE

When you have noticed what's come up, paused, and asked some probing questions, you'll likely arrive at a powerful moment of awareness. At this moment, you'll probably catch a glimpse of what could be different or how the pattern in play has impacted your life. At this moment, you'll likely feel empowered by your ability to notice and inquire and have a healthy desire for *more*.

Here, you'll probably have just enough insight, along with a growing sense of confidence and self-trust, that prompts you to say: *"I am going to make a change at this moment. In facing this familiar and depleting pattern, I am going to remember my power rests right here, within me, and I am going to make a more conscious choice. Right now, I am going to do something differently."*

Just as with your intuition and spirit guidance, when you pair the insights derived from this personal process with action, you're able to transform your life. When you understand, or even simply have a sense of, what's at work within you, you're then able to make choices from an empowered and informed place. This is how you build a life congruent with your Soul.

Life is a series of arising awareness and choice-based responses. When you welcome awareness and build your relationship with it, you're better able to respond from a grounded, informed, healthy place.

If you can accept this process and take responsibility for it, you clarify the lines of communication between you and your Soul. Your body may no longer need to ache when you finally ask it, *"What is this pain, and how am I meant to work with it to gain a greater understanding of myself?"* Your psyche might no longer need to nag you with dreams if you acknowledge the persistent themes being presented and consciously agree to begin looking at them. You may no longer feel lost in relationships when you stop and ask yourself, *"What about this pattern wants to teach me something? What do I need to learn in this repetitive cycle? What fears or wounds of mine keep repeating in my relationships?"*

Don't underestimate the value of simply making a different, more conscious choice. When you become aware of a rising emotion or a pattern, you then have the ability to stop and choose to respond differently than you have in the past. There is intrinsic value in acknowledging that what you've been choosing or doing has perpetuated a difficult pattern and consciously deciding to do something other than that. You don't need to know what the perfect choice or decision is, you can simply start with doing something that breaks the old, tired, unhealthy pattern.

 ## SACRED INTENTION-SETTING:
Your Personal Practice of Responsibility

This process of noticing, inquiring, reflecting, and choosing will be uniquely personal. For some, these concepts are brand-new and will take time to understand and integrate fully. For others, this material is familiar and will serve to encourage more in-depth personal exploration. Wherever you are with this process (even if you're right now simply inclined to look at it from a distance, considering whether it's right for you), it's important to honor that. And so, let's create a place next to your Soul Fire for your practice of personal responsibility.

When you're ready, read silently or aloud this intention:

Breathing and centering, I return my attention to my Soul Fire. As I return to this place, I feel its familiar warmth and comfort. I feel its perennial invitation to sit, reflect, take stock, and rest.

Here, right now, I intend to create a space next to my Soul Fire for my personal responsibility practice. This might look like a small altar or mantel, a seat or vessel, or a ball of energy or light. Here, I create a space that reminds me of the awesome power of taking personal responsibility and a space within which to bring and look at what I've discovered in my own practice of accountability.

This space of personal practice offers me opportunities to rest, reflect, learn, make connections, ask for and receive guidance, and honor my fears, worries, and confusion. I know that this practice of personal responsibility will challenge me, and so I may come to this place during those times. This place is entirely loving, supportive, guiding, and nourishing. Here, there is no judgment. Here, there is love, curiosity, and recognition.

**POWERING INTENTION
WITH ACTION**

Consider your own comfort level with creating and then visiting this place of personal responsibility you've built next to your Soul Fire. Might you visit this place weekly? Every few days? Even daily? How would that look? What's doable for you? How can this place support you as you work with personal responsibility in your life?

The Power of Free Will and Choice

Your power resides within you. What you make of it—who you are—lies in your choices. *You* are your own creation; *you* get to choose what you do and who you are. As a Soul and a human being, you are responsible for your relationship with the power of choice. This relationship can set you free.

Standing in your power means carrying the knowledge, even when it's hard or painful or confusing, that your choices are supreme. It means accepting that your power of choice and your power of free will are creating your experience, moment by moment. That, in each moment, what you *choose* can alter, refine, shift, or improve your reality.

> *"Between stimulus and response, there is a space.*
> *In that space is our power to choose our response.*
> *In our response lies our growth and our freedom."*
>
> —Viktor E. Frankl

You are responsible for your relationship with the powers of choice and free will. Even if you never acknowledge or accept that this is true, these universal forces are still alive and well within you. Choosing to ignore them is a refusal to take responsibility; not accepting them is an abdication of your spiritual self. Why? Because what's within you projects itself out and into the theater of your life, whether you insert yourself into that process or not.

This is why numbing, ignoring, self-medicating with the aim of not feeling, and refusing to acknowledge pain or dysfunction is so ineffective. This is why, in a society that rewards not feeling or acknowledging what's held within, we experience destruction and suffering. People who are unconscious project the unhealed parts of themselves into the outside world. The pain and destruction we see around us reflect the unhealed wounds carried within humanity.

We are creating our reality in every moment and have the power to choose what we embody in ourselves and therefore contribute to the world around us.

The value of one healed person is profound and magnificent, and this is why personal responsibility is a sacred value and act. When you stop unconsciously projecting your wounded self into the world, and instead, choose to tend to and heal yourself, you are doing your part to uplift and heal humanity. You are choosing to stop the unconscious passing on of anger, pain, blame, and dysfunction and instead are contributing self-aware, high-vibrating presence. You're cleaning up humanity's energetic playing field.

This is evolution, growth, and enlightenment. When you know, accept, understand, and choose to live in accordance with this, to the best of your ability, you are doing your divine part. It's a sacred service to yourself and to humanity.

A Message from the Other Side

"Remember who you are, and particularly, who you choose to be, in your most difficult moments. Remember, when you feel most burdened, that you have the power to choose who you are. You, at any moment, can choose divine support for yourself. Call us and we will come, in support and in love. Use the power of conscious choice to lift yourself above the seeming chaos of the human life and into the light, stillness, and loving center of the Soul."

The Gifts of Personal Responsibility

Personal responsibility is perhaps the most significant predictor of success on the Soul journey. That is, the more you're willing to take responsibility for yourself and build a life from that place, the more aligned with your Soul you'll become.

There are sacred gifts that come from embracing personal responsibility: vibrancy, grounding, grace when you make mistakes and need to adjust, and a deep knowing that you're in control of yourself, no matter how chaotic the world becomes. You'll also experience more robust and more evident connections to your intuition and your Spirit Team as you step into personal responsibility.

When you're committed to living in alignment with your Soul, through personal responsibility, you'll experience greater clarity about your life and how your experiences inform, shape, and inspire you. You'll cultivate an ever-increasing understanding of your personal power and your intrinsic ability to heal, honor, and take sacred care of yourself.

Living with personal responsibility, you'll experience the comfort that comes from knowing you're divinely held and guided, and harness the glorious ah-ha moments that lead you to step into your power.

As your ability to take responsibility and create a practice around that grows, you'll find that you naturally engage more effectively with your intuition and your Spirit Guides. These divine forces of reassurance remind you of the power of single moments of choice and action and applaud your progress, offering in-kind guidance and confirmation.

Their emphasis isn't on arriving at an outcome; instead, these friendly divine forces relish the distinct opportunities to bring about an ah-ha moment or impart a sudden insight that unlocks greater awareness. All it takes is a moment, a word, an act, a movement of the wind in the trees, a look from a stranger, or a line in a poem, to ignite deep awareness and change you forever. They love to confirm and affirm, especially when you've made a brave choice, come upon some transformational place of healing, or stepped into your power. Your guides live for this stuff—*they love it.*

Be present and aware, so your guides can reach you. Slow down, notice the sacred, indulge intuitive hunches, open your mind and heart in curiosity, wonder, and faith. Value the single acts of personal responsibility that you can engage in each day and know, deep within your being, that these moments represent open portals between you and the divine.

When you're observant about what's happening within you, aware of patterns or narratives, and committed to making conscious change, you are inherently more reachable. When you're in that place, your intuition and Spirit Guides will find you, each and every time. In that place, the gifts of personal responsibility are yours to receive.

SACRED INTENTION-SETTING:
Connecting with the Powers of Choice and Free Will

It's useful to pause and reflect on how you're reacting and responding to what you're reading. Does it resonate? Do you feel some resistance? What wants to come along with you immediately? What do you need to take some more time considering? Let's take this approach with the powers of choice and free will. Let's look at your relationship with these forces and how you might deepen that relationship.

When you're ready, read silently or aloud this intention:

I open to discovering where in my body my powers of choice and free will reside. I notice any physical sensations or intuitive guidance I get regarding where in my body these forces are held.

As I notice my body and these forces, I am curious about my current relationship with the powers of choice and free will. Do I accept these powers of choice and free will? Are there places in my life where I do not accept them? Are there situations, relationships, or challenges currently in my life where using my powers of choice and free will could purify, heal, or transform what I'm experiencing? How might I deepen my understanding of choice and free will and take additional responsibility for using those forces within my life?

I am curious about any resistance I have to these forces, and I welcome those insights so that I might consider them. I ask my Soul, through my intuition, to illuminate or guide me to the spaces in my life where choice and free will could transform and heal me.

POWERING INTENTION
WITH ACTION

Consider what's come up for you in this exercise and what you're willing to do about it. Does the power of choice fire you up and make you ready to clear what's blocking you? Does the power of free will make you anxious or feel daunted? Wherever you are, consider the next right step in your journey to becoming more responsible for your choices and free will. Consider what you might do today or this week that would reflect your power of conscious choice and grounded free will. What small change could you make today that helps you reclaim your power? What choice wants to be made so that you are taking better care of yourself?

"Your task is not to seek for love, but merely to seek and find all the barriers within yourself that you have built against it."

—Rumi

———————————————— ♥ ————————————————

"If you restore balance in your own self, you will be contributing immensely to the healing of the world."

—Deepak Chopra

Chapter Five

Life with Your Soul: Courage, Change, and Self-Love

Taking exquisite care of yourself is divine. It's sacred. It's personally responsible. When you love and value yourself enough to prioritize your journey to become more conscious and aware of who and what you are, you have done it—you've cracked the divine code.

To take personal responsibility is to love yourself. To do what, at times, feels hard, is to offer yourself the gifts of healing and evolution. Don't mistake the tough stuff for random onerousness; sometimes, what's deeply difficult is the most loving of all. Friendly forces can exist alongside challenging moments, processes, and transformations.

When you're facing and working with spiritual truths, this is, in fact, the truth: when you feel most challenged, there isn't an absence of love—there is an influx of love.

The Universe applauds bravery; it supports courage and grants divine assistance. Remember this, and, in your tough moments, remember that you are worthy of this!

You didn't come here to give away your power. You didn't come here to dissolve into the illusion that you're weak, broken, inherently flawed, and without self-direction. You came here to go on a journey to discover yourself—magnificently, thoroughly, courageously finding out who you are and then, *deciding and choosing* who you want to be and doing your best, each day, to live as that version of you.

To choose to live in alignment with your Soul—a life filled with intuition, spiritual guidance, self-inquiry, personal responsibility, and embracing your humanity as a tool to discover your spirit—is so brave. It's the highest value you can place on yourself. It's an act of fierce self-love.

You came here to remember your Soul and to love and value yourself so fiercely that you dare to live a life that reflects it.

Living this way takes commitment, practice, and intention. It requires you be patient and compassionate with yourself, granting yourself grace, forgiveness, and room to grow when needed. Living a life congruent with your Soul includes tenderness, curiosity, quiet, and reflection. It asks for resilience and a get-back-up-again attitude, and that you learn about emotions, your triggers, your wounds, and your inner world. A life aligned with your Soul will ask you to love and care for yourself with consistent kindness.

This path is both soft and fierce. It is warmly inviting and intensely daunting. It is beautifully intricate and profoundly simple. Just as there are paradoxes within us, there are paradoxes on this path—yin and yang, dark and light, simplicity and depth. You will find essential truths in those dualities; you will find yourself in those dualities.

These dualities aren't always quickly resolved, and often, they'll require you to journey, one step at a time, unable to jump ahead to an outcome or hurry things up to skip the tough parts. There's a patience and tolerance required on this path, and in those moments when you're most restless, taking good care of yourself and treating yourself with kindness is critical.

There's wisdom in remembering that, sometimes, there isn't a "right" answer or outcome at which to arrive. It's the journey through the human condition and into the dualities at work within you that ultimately change you. It's the journey into and out of transformation, which can often look confusing or dark, wherein you get to know yourself. Developing a deep understanding of yourself and the conscious and unconscious forces within you is the work. The healing comes when you embrace what you've found and let it change you—when you choose to live in alignment with what you now know about yourself and your Soul.

Living in alignment with the Soul challenges you to love yourself more unconditionally than ever. This kind of living asks you to find a way to take practical, daily, human responsibility for living with your Soul.

If spirit guidance is guaranteed because you are divinely loved, then your earthly journey includes moving toward a place where you embody self-love. The grand forces that love you without end, ask you to love yourself the same way.

On this path of self-discovery and healing, you will be asked to remember your intrinsic value, your innate spark of divine light, and then, to take care of that inner source of light. Living here, you'll be asked to build a courageous—but practical—practice of self-love in your life, taking good care of yourself, and accepting responsibility for keeping your Soul Fire tended and nourished.

Self-Love: Restoring the Pathways to Our Soul

We know that our human experiences illuminate the pathways to our Souls. We know that we are here to find the paths that need healing, clearing, and repair so that we can live more conscious lives. When we approach those pathways intending to heal them from a place of personal responsibility and with the awareness that we are divinely supported and equipped with essential spiritual tools, we've moved into the powerful space of self-love.

When we tend to ourselves, to our Soul Fire, with dedication, we are performing acts of self-love.

Self-love will lead you, always, to your Soul.

Here, you are rooted in the seat of your power and can make intentioned, healthy, brave choices for yourself. Here, you are empowered to choose who and what you are.

We often consider self-love to be a series of indulgences: going to the spa, taking a personal day from work, or allowing yourself a nap on the weekend, for instance. Or, we believe loving ourselves to be a softer task—something that feels good but is different from hard work, accomplishment, or the rigors of daily life. We often regard self-love as optional.

These perceptions couldn't be further from the true, ever-present, spiritual nature of self-love. Most of us need a mindset shift on the irrefutable value of loving ourselves and treating ourselves with compassion.

You see, we live in a society that asks us to become separate from ourselves and to judge, doubt, and treat ourselves harshly. So many of the mainstream, popular messages we receive tell us we are inadequate, flawed, unlovable, unworthy, not good enough. Many of our systems, from religious to educational, from governmental to the familial, are rooted in the belief that humans are inherently flawed and need to be controlled or at least carefully managed. We are taught not to trust ourselves and to water down our uniqueness to be granted inclusion in the comfortable norm. It's a groupthink that ignores spiritual truths and devalues the human spirit.

And, so, in this kind of environment, no wonder self-love is regarded as indulgent or even selfish. No wonder walking a path of existential self-discovery, healing, and empowerment is considered outlandish, crazy, or a rejection of mainstream, "normal" society.

How many times have you heard someone say they feel guilty for taking care of themselves? How many times have you felt guilty for taking care of yourself? How many times have you worried you'd be regarded as crazy or silly for doing something spiritual? How often do you hide your spiritual curiosity, practice, and self? How often do you abandon yourself in favor of belonging? How many times have you ignored or suppressed your intuition because you were afraid it would cost you inclusion, belonging, approval, or value?

You aren't alone. So many of us do it. It's scary to be true to our spiritual selves; it can cost us the trappings of the "safe" and "secure" human life to be true to our Souls. This kind of living isn't for the faint of heart—it's for the brave, the resilient, the ones who believe that, despite the costs, alignment with self-truth is the only way to live.

Society would have you believe that you can't handle this kind of living. But you can—*oh yes, you can.*

Within our society, daring to act in accordance with your Soul is an act of defiance. To choose to love yourself and to prioritize yourself is an act of defiance. To regard yourself and the advancement of your consciousness as your most important job, worthy of devoted investment, is downright rebellious. Courageous self-love isn't embarking on a series of spa visits; it's about the brave choice to deem yourself so valuable that you heal yourself, invest in your evolution, and explore and understand your inner depths. Courageous self-love is about taking personal responsibility so steadfastly that you can't help but purify your life and what you're offering the world.

Never underestimate the value of one healed person standing, grounded and brave, within their Soul. Never underestimate the magnitude of that light, and the permission it grants others to tell their truth and shine. One healed person makes a profound impact on society, the world, the planet, and the Universe. That one person isn't someone else—it's you.

This isn't easy. It can feel hard. Really hard. But loving yourself enough to heal yourself is the highest calling there is. It's the grandest desire of your Soul.

And you don't have to be perfect! Love is an evolutionary force; it refines, polishes, offers space, and is perpetually forgiving. Deciding to operate from a place of self-love will include moments of negative self-talk, skepticism, and self-doubt—and that's okay. Self-love is an effort you make, improving as you are able, and restoring when it's waned. There isn't a finish line or moment of pinnacle achievement; it's a process of refining your relationship with yourself and endeavoring, in the long run, to be kind, supportive, forgiving, and compassionate to yourself more often than you are not.

This is why healing is an act of self-love: as you learn about yourself and what makes you what and who you are, you'll develop empathy and understanding for your journey, and you are then more likely to allow yourself to grow, correct, and make new choices. When you understand yourself in a kind and empathetic way, you are better able to coach and love yourself to the next best version of you.

The choice to love yourself and to put steady, intentioned, honest effort into that endeavor is the most potent and profound choice you'll ever make.

When you do, inevitably, it will lead to a powerful and profound transformation in your own life and the lives of others. That choice of self-love raises the vibration of the collective—*of the all*. The choice of self-love sets your compass to the true north of your Soul and makes you a conscious, responsible, loving citizen of the Universe.

The Truth: An Intimidating Ally

The place where personal responsibility meets insight often feels incredibly refreshing. When you discover a truth, one that jives with your intuition or is validated by spirit guidance, there's usually a moment of profound relief. And it feels good! Even if what brought you here hasn't felt so good or you aren't yet sure about what's to come, this place of the ah-ha or the profound insight, feels *good*.

You deserve this place. This is the place where you come into deep alignment with this new truth, where you feel its accuracy in your body. You see how it fits right into your history, and it illuminates corners of your earlier life previously obscured or clouded. You see how this truth offers irrefutable insight into how you've been operating or what you've been assuming or how you've been selling yourself short.

This truth is right. It's accurate. It has a place in your history, your present, and your future. This truth belongs to you. This truth must come *with* you, informing your choices, actions, and your life path. This truth and the discovery of it feel triumphant!

And, as lovely, exhilarating, or relief-giving as this ah-ha feels, now, as this truth begs to come along for the rest of your ride, things might begin to feel more somber. This is where what you've privately discovered will demand to be made public—or at least integrated prominently into your life. This is where the discovery of a truth morphs into a need for action. Here, that freedom of truth just might turn into a fear of change, and it might be enticing to forget the whole darn thing.

How do you *actually* do this? What will people think? What does this mean for your relationships? What does this mean for your career? How can you afford to do this? How can you upend your life? Doesn't your Soul know that you have a mortgage to pay, rent to make? Doesn't your Soul know that you can't let down your mother or your brother or your spouse? Doesn't your Soul understand that this doesn't feel safe?

Yes. Yes, your Soul knows. The Universe knows. You're human, and big change is daunting, even terrifying. It's going to roil every unconscious part of you, stirring up your fears like a wizard building a fireball in his bare hands.

But you can't forget it. You couldn't even if you tried. You see, once you know a truth, you cannot unknow it. Truth doesn't recede, even when it makes you nervous.

Feel the fear—it's okay to be daunted—and then, use the forces of self-love and courage to pair this new truth with action and change.

When you make a conscious choice to change your actions, thoughts, or behaviors so they are in greater alignment with what you know is right, best, or healthiest for you, that's the moment healing occurs. When you choose to break a lifelong pattern, stop an old, limiting behavior or train of thought, or opt to do something new and different instead of what you've always done, you are evolving. When the insights you've gathered influence your choices and actions for the better, this is the moment of healing. Here, you are no longer the same. You are transformed.

And it's right that you're not the same. You shouldn't be. It's right that your life has shifted because you now know something new. You have experienced something that cuts right to the marrow of existence, and it's wrenched you open, turned you inside out, and flushed out what's no longer accurate or real.

This is where you must remember some beautiful, divine truths:

You are not alone.

Your Soul doesn't lead you astray.

You can do this.

You have the tools, inner strength, and power to change.

You have the gift of time to consider, learn, and grow.

You are divinely held in this process.

Inconvenient Truths:
The Courage to Change

You are inherently, fundamentally, worthy of living in congruence with your Soul. You are worthy of healing and transformation. You are allowed to, at any moment, on any day, decide to stop old patterns and narratives that no longer work for you and step into a new way of being. You may choose to change anything in you at any time.

> *If knowing that you and your life are yours to direct is the key, then choosing to love yourself enough to take responsibility to make appropriate changes is the unlocking action.*

Living this way—as a person who takes responsibility for self-reflection and change—takes courage. Big courage. Why? Because change is, at least, challenging, and, at most, wrenching.

Living this way is courageous because when you decide to stop those old patterns and narratives, or release depleting relationships or jobs, or set new boundaries, it can come at a cost. And, at first, the price you pay might be hard to see beyond. The profound inconvenience of these deep truths you've encountered, uncovered, and admitted can make you want to stuff them right back into their boxes. Here, the place you came from—that blissful ignorance—looks awfully comfortable and even enticing.

So, let's honor this. In fact, there's nothing else you can do at this juncture. Here, you must acknowledge the gravity of these inconvenient truths and what you fear they might cost you. Here, you must honor that the change required by the admission of truth can make the whole exercise terrifying.

Change can look, frankly, like loss. Becoming different might mean shifting your relationships with family, partners, spouses, or children. Becoming different might mean your career or job must change, or that something new and transformational must begin. It might mean preparing to take a big leap that stirs up fears about money, safety, relationships, if and how you'll be judged, and self-doubt.

The change demanded by the discovery of a profound personal truth often at first feels like it will dismantle, destabilize, and shake your life's structure to its core. Honor this. It's okay. You're not weak or incapable, you're human!

You cannot heal what you don't feel; you cannot move through what you don't acknowledge. Big change is a big deal. Be kind and loving to yourself.

This is why taking good, loving care of yourself is a fundamental part of the practice of personal responsibility and change. When you get on board with taking responsibility for yourself and your life, and you start down that existential path toward greater awakening and more vibrant living, you're going to arrive at some moments that stop you in your tracks. It's here that courage and self-love get you through.

This path isn't easier, but it's rewarding. This path isn't without life-changing truth, but those truths will, ultimately, translate into peace, fulfillment, happiness, and balance. This path isn't without terrible inconvenience, but it's in those places we find our Souls—our own spiritual core.

This path requires courage and, at times, what looks like loss or high personal cost, yes. But what you receive in return for your brave spiritual work will wholly and utterly transform you. Change like this isn't easy to make in the short term, but it is decidedly more fulfilling in the long run because you'll be living in alignment with your most authentic self. You will find yourself and know yourself on the other side of this kind of courageous change. *That* is what your courage buys you: *yourself.*

Building a Relationship with Change

Of course, as we've learned about the spiritual journey, there is the acceptance of a truth, and then, there is the required action. Yes, each time you find another truth, about yourself or your Soul or the Universe, you'll then see, as you work with that truth, that it begs to be translated into action. That truth will nudge and nag you until you make it personal, real, tangible, manifest in your consciousness and your life. Truth, especially inconvenient truth, will present to you the most tender, precise, exquisite realities about yourself, and then, it will present you with the hard-to-ignore next step: *change*.

When we dig our heels in and resist what wants to change in our lives, we create imbalance.

When we refuse to acknowledge what must come or go or evolve or shift, we stand in direct opposition to the Universe. While it can be immensely difficult, even heart-wrenching, to move with change, we suffer more when we don't. Where we land—the other side of change—finds us more evolved, wise, content, and true.

The other side of change sees us closer to our spirit, our essence, our Soul.

Often, the shifts or changes we know are coming or need to be initiated in our lives, are so fear-inducing that we avoid or delay or ignore or even refuse that demand for action. Here, self-love, courage, and a deep connection to your spiritual center are transformative tools. Most of the time, that journey of change, however initially destabilizing or seemingly destructive, leads to a more vibrant, authentic, and fulfilling place of being and living.

Don't become marooned in the experience of change as loss. If you do, you'll miss the transformational and transcendent forces endeavoring to sweep through your life and make it more pure, vibrant, and authentic.

Change is a constant in the Universe. It's the law, and it challenges our humanness to the very core. It's easy to regard change as an unwelcome—even punishing—force. But it's not. The divine powers surrounding us are focused on evolution and, ultimately, designed to offer us unlimited support in our growth. The Universe's motives are pure.

And, as is the case with Universal truths, when you work with them, when you accept and allow them, you find more peace. When you live in congruence with Universal forces, you live in the sweet spot, where suffering finds purpose and evolution finds its home in you.

Change arrives with a pure motive: to restore our faith, our hope, our self-trust and self-belief, our relationship with higher divine forces, and our connection to our Souls. Change wants to propel you to a place of greater awareness.

And so, consider your relationship with change. Consider how you regard change and how you might open to change as a constant, pure, evolutionary force.

 ## SACRED INTENTION-SETTING:
Exploring Your Relationship with Change

Spend some time considering your innate reactions to what's been outlined here. Does it make you angry or frustrated? Relieved? Daunted? Reassured? Consider what comes up for you and welcome what arises. In the welcoming, you'll more deeply understand your relationship with change. When you witness your semiconscious reactions and innate responses, you then have the power to shift them. And, if a shift isn't quite ready to happen, then simply observing and accepting what happens in your body when we talk about change is a valid first step.

When you're ready, read silently or aloud this intention:

I am curious about the narratives about change I have carried throughout my life. I am curious about what I say—without even thinking—about change. When the winds of change blow in my life, how do I react? What do I do? Are there places of defensiveness, fear, or resistance? Are there places of curiosity, desire, and longing? What was I taught about change? What beliefs about change have I created throughout my life and my personal experiences? Where is there room in my life to accept, allow, and honor the force of change? Where is there room in my life to consider that change is a loving force of the Universe designed to bring about my evolution, healing, and growth?

POWERING INTENTION WITH ACTION

Consider what comes up for you in this exercise; consider the areas that beg further investigation or understanding. Consider how you might deepen your relationship with change. Consider how you might forgive change for its impact in your life, rooting out the spaces where you've blamed this Universal force for something in your life that's occurred. Consider where change has brought you gifts, even in the most difficult of circumstances.

Allow, Accept, and Surrender

There are fundamental tenets of change; axioms that, when embraced, can make change seem less arbitrary, painful, and disruptive. These pillars of change—allow, accept, and surrender—offer accessible, practical ways to regard and work with this divine force.

That saying, "You cannot change what you don't accept"—the one you've heard before? Well, it's true. It's a principle of the Universe. When we don't accept what's occurring, we create a stalemate with reality. And yes, "reality" is entirely subjective and could spawn its own deeply philosophical conversation, but here we are talking about the reality, or the truth, of what's occurring in front of you, in your life.

When you can acknowledge that something is happening, especially when you don't like it, you energetically shift yourself from a place of disbelieving stalemate into centered power.

A helpful way to approach fear around a difficult truth is to state it out loud. State out loud your deepest fear, or the harshest truth, or whatever you're struggling to accept. Say it out loud and feel it in your body; feel the emotions around it, feel any resistance or blocks, feel where your power might be within this statement, and notice any relief or pressure-lifting that arise.

When you state something out loud, you take it out of your body. You remove it from the inner, semiconscious realms, and transplant it, definitively, into your conscious, working reality. You cannot engage with anything you have not looked in the eye. Not effectively, at least.

These are truths that can be disruptive, yes, but when ignored, numbed, suppressed, or disavowed, they only gain strength and cause suffering until they're acknowledged. What's buried within us plays out in our lives and around us until we consciously take control.

And so, even if it devastates you, or roils deep-seated emotions, or fills you with fear, say it out loud. Admit it to yourself, bravely. Allow it into your space. Bring what you're feeling to your conscious awareness so that, ultimately, you can move into acceptance. Acceptance will grant you the ability to make whatever change or shift is necessary for your emotional health, growth, and well-being.

Accept it to shift it.

This process will immediately grant you relief. Even if for a few moments. There will be relief that you've allowed yourself to admit a persistent truth. There will be hope that you have or could now move into a place of accepting this new truth. You don't have to like, in any way, what you've allowed or accepted, but because accepting shifts you into your power, you can now choose to do something that honors and heals.

Shame, guilt, and fear live in the shadows. The things that cause us the most significant emotional roadblocks—that bind our feet, choke our voices, and deplete our energies—thrive on secrecy. Dare to trust your Soul, your divinity, and declare, out loud, what resides in the secret shadows. Bring it up and accept it. It won't destroy you. It'll set you free.

Then, surrender.

You cannot control what has occurred. You cannot direct the forces of life and the Universe to your liking and comfort. The cycles of ebb and flow, death and rebirth, march on, without regard for our like or dislike of them.

Surrendering the need to control or direct—surrendering the illusion that you could even do so—will free you. Your power is in your response. It's in your choice and free will. Your power is in how thoroughly you allow the forces of change and evolution to influence and permeate your life. You cannot control these forces, but you can surrender to them, permitting them to inform, inspire, and transform you.

> *Surrender isn't giving away your power. Instead, it's acknowledging where in the process your power lies: in the response and action you choose.*

When you work with these axioms of change, you automatically recalibrate your energy. You're more reachable by your Spirit Guides, and your intuition will feel sharper and clearer—and likely more comfortable to follow.

The truth is going to heal you. Telling yourself the truth—accepting, allowing, and surrendering to the truth—is the mindset game-changer.

 ## SACRED INTENTION-SETTING:
Allowing, Accepting, and Surrendering in Your Life

Spend some time considering how you have experienced the axioms of change (allow, accept, and surrender) in your life. Are these new concepts to you? Or perhaps universal truths you endeavor to work with regularly? Because we're human and we have very active inner monologues, it's reasonable to experience some resistance to these ideas and to be inclined to come up with exceptions to these rules. Honor what comes up, even if it feels argumentative, and then, work it through. Challenge yourself to try on allowing or accepting or surrendering for size and see how it shifts your perspective or feels in your body.

When you're ready, read silently or aloud this intention:

I open to the Universal forces of allowing, acceptance, and surrender. I welcome insight about a situation or experience in my life where allowing, acceptance, or surrender could help me. What situation or experience could become clearer if I accept it?

What situation or experience could improve if I surrendered to it? How might my suffering be relieved or my worry dissipate or a holding pattern release if I brought in the concepts of allowing, acceptance, and surrender? What could I gain from doing so?

What does it cost me when I do not accept, allow, or surrender? I offer myself compassion and patience as I explore these topics and practice working with these forces.

POWERING INTENTION
WITH ACTION

Consider a situation, problem, persistent theme, experience, or concern you're dealing with and how accepting, allowing, or surrendering could offer relief, a shift, or empowerment. Practice it. Simply try it on for size: What would it feel like to accept what's happening? What would it feel like to surrender to it? What does it do for your mind, your body, your emotional state, when you simply accept what's happening? How could you be intentional and conscious in accepting, allowing, and surrendering to the realities in your life? How could doing so shift you into a place of personal power and intention?

Making Change Doable:
Take One Right Step

It's physics, Universal law, that an object at rest remains at rest and an object in motion remains in motion. There is deep, intrinsic value in movement, even the smallest of movement, because it connects us to hope, faith, glimpses of a better future, personal power, and resilience. We are much better able to remember and see that we are buoyant and resilient when we are engaged in action. Action positions us to recognize our spiritual nature.

Why is this?

Firstly, because movement and action fan the flame of the Soul. Whether small, intentioned steps or grand leaps—or even thoughtful, chosen times of rest—action requires alignment with our path. Those small steps, even when you're most overwhelmed or doubtful or fearful, require a tiny spark of hope. The grand leaps, as daunting and knee-knocking as they are, awaken a deep-seated knowing. And, those chosen, intentional rests require awareness that there is more ahead and that a pause or break will power future movement toward that "more."

Action connects you to the flame within your Soul, it nourishes that flame, and it deepens your sense of personal resilience, self-trust, and intuition.

When these action steps pay off and the ah-ha moment, the "reward," or the next horizon comes into view, that connection between your Soul, your intuition, and your conscious humanness strengthens. It's in those moments that profound alignment becomes more permanent and less shakable. You'll look back on the win you just experienced and know, *"If I did that, then I can do this,"* or *"That series of small steps led to this huge breakthrough, let me try that again."* When that faithfulness of action, even in the darkest of times, becomes your go-to, you'll experience shifts and changes that build new seats of self-trust, resilience, self-awareness, and peace within your being.

You deserve this.

You deserve to feel those payoffs, gather those insights, and engineer your life. You deserve to feel that greater alignment, the thrill of finding a part of yourself, and the knowledge that you are capable of addressing what comes at you in life.

You deserve to trust yourself implicitly. You deserve to know the fulfillment that comes when you take one right step that's congruent with the truth you know about your life and your path. You deserve to experience the fact that life doesn't have to be so harsh and that not everything requires hard work. You deserve to remember that divinity and magic are omnipresent, and when you act like they are, even if acting like that brings up fears, you connect yourself to those forces.

Adopting new and unprecedented means of self-love, self-care, and self-compassion means beginning with one small thing: that one right, safe, appropriate step you can take in honor of shifting an old pattern or breaking a depleting habit.

There is deep intrinsic value in taking the next right step. One step is powerful. It's enough. It focuses you in the present, right where your power sits. It builds momentum and restores self-trust.

Single steps make change accessible—doable—while offering you a chance to acquaint yourself with parts of you that are brave, hopeful, curious, and steadfast. Single steps remind us of the way the Universe operates and aims to teach us about how gloriously powerful we are; how it's the small, conscious, intentioned choices that transform our lives and the world. The art of the single step is sacred and a demonstration of your Soul at work in your life.

When you've allowed change to sweep into your life, noting what it's bringing or what it's demanding be released, or you've discovered a truth about yourself or found a place that needs healing, you'll soon find yourself faced with the need to take action. Here, take that next right step. Don't worry about fast and furiously advancing to the outcome. *Instead, simply choose to do the next right thing.*

The next right thing might be asking for some space or taking a break within a relationship. It might be accepting that while a more significant health issue has presented itself, your power today is in eating one healthy meal or drinking more water.

Sometimes, the next right thing might be to reach out to your tried-and-true therapist because some old trauma has been resurfacing for you, and you value the work the two of you previously did on that issue. Sometimes, the next right thing is to take some quiet time to think about a problem, while other times, what's necessary is to step into looking at a problem in a new way. There are times that the next right step is to choose to turn an old, tired narrative on its head and declare that you're no longer going to assume you can't get ahead, or that you aren't good enough, or that you won't find what you're looking for.

Sometimes, the next right thing is quiet, reflective, paused. Other times, that next step is active, fierce, determined, and bold. And still, there is much middle ground here, where intentioned single steps look task-oriented, not-so-sexy, or dutiful.

Whatever the action might be, centering yourself in the power of the present moment and asking, *"What is the next right step?"* builds your relationship with change.

This place of mindful awareness and self-inquiry will remind you of your innate power of choice and offer you the comfort that comes when you choose to make brave changes in honor of your self-care.

This practice builds momentum, too.

You can choose, each day, to change something within yourself or your world. You can decide to shift something small or large, something habitual or less familiar. You can choose to remove or delete, improve or add, something from your life or routines. You can give change a try, doing so with the full intention of evaluating the outcome and without commitment to its permanence. You can try something different with the aim to alter a pattern or shift a theme or get ahold of a pesky self-defeating narrative.

When you're open to change and even "play" with change, observing what shifts or is altered in your life when you implement something new, you're in the zone of sacred action. You're working with the Universe. You're working with your Soul. You're the outfielder in the baseball game, staying loose and ready for the fly ball. There's value in being familiar with change and in building a give-and-take relationship with change. There's value in "staying loose" but grounded in yourself.

You can decide, at any time and as often as you'd like, to step into change, greeting it as a friendly tool with which to engineer your best life. You can choose to get to know yourself as someone who allows the forces of change to bring what they will, even if what transpires is painful or seemingly without merit. You have the power to stay in your body, anchor in conscious choice, and ask your Soul, *"How might I work with change today?"*

The Power of Release

Sometimes, the change required for our growth and evolution demands we let go of something: a pattern, routine, or tradition; an assumption, narrative, or outdated belief; a relationship, career track, or old comfort. Sometimes, change asks us to release attachment to something comfortable to propel us out of the familiar and ordinary and into a place of growth and evolution.

In this way, change doesn't always need to feel like a gathering of gumption to create something new, or like a burst of sudden, decisive forward movement. Sometimes, that next right step is letting something go.

And while that sounds simple, it can be incredibly difficult.

As humans, we are comforted by and drawn to the familiar. Of course, there are times that "familiar" isn't necessarily healthy for us, and it holds us back from admitting some truth or from taking a chance. There are times, too, that the familiar is just fine; a loving relationship, a nourishing self-care practice, or a career that suits us well. Just because something is familiar doesn't mean it's bad—or good—but familiar, to most of us, is comforting, which is why letting go or releasing it can be so difficult.

There are times we don't have a choice. The winds of change seem to sweep into our lives and alter our course forever. We didn't ask for it; we never wanted to live *this* way. But here we are. And there's nothing to do but accept what has happened and choose to let go.

When we try to hold something together or keep something in place that needs to dissolve, shift, or come apart, we're getting in the way of the Universe. Here, you'll create suffering for yourself. Here, your fear of change or of what life will be like on the other side of this shift has taken over. Here, the human illusions will let you down and cost you alignment with your Soul.

This is where surrender is essential: as humans, we assume we know better. But we don't. We often aren't privy to the full picture because of our inherent fears, aversions to change, and penchant for comfort. Sometimes, we just can't see the wisdom of an end. Sometimes, that nearly unconscious drive to not quit or not give up or to perform duty, responsibility, or loyalty gets squarely in our way. Sometimes, it's in our highest and best honor that something dissolves or goes away. Sometimes, we deplete ourselves and cause suffering because we are opposing the natural forces of release.

"When I let go of what I am,
I become what I might be."

—Lao Tzu

Furthermore, there are times when life simply feels overwhelming, and the next right step is to release *just one thing*. Clearing one log from a vast logjam is profoundly valuable. That one action of release can create movement, space, and breathing room for new insights or solutions. Sometimes, removing that one log from the logjam helps to get the other stuck logs moving. Sometimes, in the absence of knowing what we "should do," there's value in identifying what no longer is right or appropriate, what no longer belongs or works, and releasing it. There are times the "no" is more evident than the "yes" and so removing what no longer belongs helps clear the path ahead. Particularly when you're overwhelmed or if there are many things in your life demanding change, adopting the practice of releasing what no longer belongs or is no longer right or true is relief-giving, empowering, and practically useful.

Sometimes, the lesson for us is to see that we are futilely attempting to control what we cannot possibly control, and that releasing changes the whole picture.

We can become the logjam when we endeavor to hold onto something or maintain something that isn't meant to be. And so, consider that release might look like pausing your effort to keep something together, and simply let the situation be just as it is. Sometimes, release asks you to stop attempting to direct, control, assume, predict, maintain, sustain, or manage. Sometimes, it's our human fears and assumptions—showing up as control—that are causing the block and taking a step back is necessary to allow the natural forces of life to do as they will.

There are times that release is remembering that we don't have the full picture, and we don't know better, despite our human ego's assertions that we do. There are moments when release requires remembering there is something much larger at work in the Universe and choosing to stop acting out of fear and instead step, as best we can, into a place of faith and trust.

Give yourself permission to stop working so hard to direct life events, and simply allow, release, and have faith in what comes. Love yourself enough to trust these universal forces.

A Message from the Other Side

"What often stands in our way is releasing what no longer works for us or feeds us or honors us. Often we know what could be, but we're fearful of letting go of what is. These aren't quandaries for the faint of heart, but the courageous are rewarded with vibrancy and fulfillment and wholeness. Release in faith and then receive the new things that line up in congruence with who you are."

SACRED INTENTION-SETTING:
What Wants to Be Released?

Let's pause to sit with this notion of release. Small or large, there are surely things in your life that are ready to be let go or released. If you're curious about what some of these might be, you can work with this intention.

When you're ready, read silently or aloud this intention:

I welcome the notion of release into my consciousness. I am curious about what the force of release might teach me or bring me. I am ready to receive insight about one area of my life where release could improve, heal, shift, or empower me.

I settle into awareness about a situation, theme, event, or dynamic in my life in which I am trying to assert control when it might be best to release and simply let things be as they are. I settle into awareness of what releasing that desire to control could bring me or teach me.

I open up to understand what could be mine if I release something that no longer serves me. I look with compassion on any resistance or fear that arises in me as I consider releasing. I welcome in any feelings of relief, empowerment, perspective-shifting, or peace that come when I consider releasing what no longer serves me.

**POWERING INTENTION
WITH ACTION**

What could you consider releasing? What have you been trying to control or direct, to no avail? Where is your desire to hang on causing you pain, suffering, and anguish? Where in your life might there be a logjam that could benefit from you releasing just one log? What one right step can you take in this moment toward being ready to release what is holding you back?

The Anatomy of the Big Leap

As is the case with the human journey, there are times when small, intentioned steps are necessary, or a deep, reflective rest is required—and there are times when there is nothing to do but leap.

You know this place. This is a place that will not be denied. You usually arrive here after lots of truth-telling (to yourself and some trusted others), a series of good and right single steps, lots of reflection and consideration, a healthy dose of fear and doubt, and a core intuition that *it's time* and *you'll be okay.*

Each of us, in our lifetimes, will arrive at these precipices of significant change—often several times in our lives. These are the moments where we take the biggest gambles: on ourselves, on our faith, on the Universe, on our spiritual nature. When we do this—when we leap— we catapult forward on our Soul journey. We align, more brilliantly than before, with our Soul. Here, we learn to trust ourselves in one grand motion. Here, we learn that our process has been sound and grounded.

Here, we receive proof that miracles and divine intervention happen, and that we are extensions of the spiritual nature of the Universe.

And it's almost required, don't you think? That each of us takes a handful of these huge leaps in our lives? It seems that these tests of faith and exercises of personal power are written into our blueprints. If that's the case, then it makes this process of intentioned step-taking even more valuable. You don't arrive at this moment of leaping lightly or by surprise. No, you know it's coming. You sense it and live with it—and all of the fear and doubt it dredges up. The journey to your Soul and the intentioned process of becoming more conscious is designed to not only get you through the walk but prepare you for the moments of grand advancement.

When you've stayed faithfully with the process of re-discovering your Soul, you've prepared for these big leaps.

The Gift of Healing: Self-Trust

One of the greatest gifts of this process of evolution and change is self-trust. When you embark on the journey of the Soul, gathering the tools offered you, opening up to divine guidance and intuition, and welcoming in the forces of personal responsibility, change, action, acceptance, and surrender, you learn to trust yourself.

For so many of us, this is life-changing.

For so many of us, life experiences, whether in early childhood or throughout adulthood, create gaps in our perceptions of ourselves, our power, capabilities, and self-trust. It's so easy to take in a painful life event as a personal failure or confirmation that you're not capable. It can go unnoticed that as we journey through life experiences, we begin to doubt or mistrust ourselves.

So when we look truth in the eye, accepting and surrendering, and step into our personal powers of choice and free will to greet change as a friend, we rebuild our relationship with ourselves.

Self-trust builds when we take care of ourselves, meeting our needs, and healing our wounds. Self-trust grows when we create routines, habits, and practices that nourish us. Self-trust expands when we talk kindly to ourselves, offering grace and self-forgiveness when we don't know better, and endeavor to stay on the Soul path.

Self-trust arises when we value growth and evolution over perfection, when we love ourselves unconditionally and supportively.

Accepting personal responsibility and pairing it with action is the life force of self-trust. We can trust ourselves when we know we can recognize signs and signals in our lives that point us to our own inner landscape. When you trust your intuition and pair that with action, you immediately build self-trust, and when you receive spiritual guidance and allow it to inform your choices and perspectives, you are tending to the sacred place of self-trust.

This beautiful by-product of rebuilding self-trust creates momentum and awareness of its own. This entire process is so deeply interconnected that doing one piece of it impacts and uplifts every other point in the cycle.

Your seat of truth lives right within you. When you deeply and sacredly trust yourself to live in congruence with your spiritual center, you're able to build a life aligned with your Soul. When you cultivate a deep trust in yourself, you more permanently align with your personal power and sacred agency.

A Message from the Other Side

"Remember who you are, and particularly who you choose to be. Remember that you always have the power to choose who you are. When you respond from deeper and greater awareness, you transcend and evolve, lifting yourself above the seeming chaos of the human experience and toward the light, stillness, and loving center of the Soul."

Change Requires Pause, Quiet, and Rest

It's important to note here that movement and action can also look like stopping, pausing, and taking a deep dive. Progress isn't always linear. Often, it's going to look like going deep down and within rather than propelling yourself forward toward a desired outcome. Healing and conscious change require stopping to feel difficult emotions, spending time talking or processing, engaging in guided meditation or trauma clearing, or intentionally reducing busyness and clutter to sit in silence or quiet reflection.

Pause, quiet, and rest count as action on this journey.

The importance of your emotional, cognitive, and spiritual processes here cannot be overstated. When you're visiting something that's been with you for a long time, it's essential to give yourself space, compassion, patience, and kindness. You might feel that pausing your life, to whatever extent, to take a deep dive, feels an awful lot like being stuck or heading into the darkness. Yes, it can feel that way, and frankly, when you're in pursuit of a life that aligns with your Soul, you *will* feel that way at times. Accepting and allowing for this will lead you to act more compassionately toward yourself, and you'll be less likely to skip or miss depth or self-discovery that's important.

Furthermore, when something painful, tragic, or shocking occurs in real time in your life, it's nearly impossible to move straight into action. Sure, you might respond or react, but please don't force a process of movement or action before its time. Remember that grieving, emotional processing, contemplative reflection, and deep rest and recovery are fundamentally necessary in life. We cannot experience something jarring and immediately step onto some pathway to enlightenment. We must experience what's occurred and feel what we feel so we can move through it.

We cannot heal what we don't feel. We cannot skip the experiences of life in favor of crossing the finish line of enlightenment. We need to be in and feel our experiences so we can ultimately process them and understand how they have changed us.

The High Five from Your Spirit Team

As you step more consciously into the process of healing and working with Universal evolutionary forces, you'll need support. This means finding the processes, methods, experiences, environments, and relationships that help you look within, discover what needs attention, and do that work. For some, that's traditional therapy or spiritual coaching; for others, it's a sound yoga practice and ample time in nature; and for some, it's energy work or working with animals.

Spirit Guides and Souls on the Other Side often implore the humans they're guiding to embrace healing activities and processes and challenge them to commit to becoming more self-aware and conscious.

There's a reason your loved ones and Spirit Guides are talking to you, and it extends far beyond wanting to confirm life after death—they want to inspire you to heal.

Your guides want to remind you why you're really here and to facilitate, if possible, ah-ha moments and paradigm shifts that bring about awakening, self-awareness, and growth in you.

When you take responsibility for your free will and embrace your power of choice, you're meeting the powers that be halfway. When you allow, accept, and surrender to truth and change, your Spirit Guides come rushing in. In taking up the work of healing and becoming more conscious, you're entering into a deep and sacred partnership with the Universe and your team of guides. You are essentially saying, *"I'm on board. I may not know exactly where I'm headed, but I'm on board, and I'm willing to take full responsibility for myself."*

You are alerting powerful benevolent forces that you are ready to be a conscious partner in your own healing and growth. This is what your guides and loved ones are after—this is why they show up. This is the winning moment!

A Message from the Other Side

"Your loved ones on the Other Side and your Spirit Guides arrive to lead you to greater conscious awareness. When you can regard change as a natural force in your life and open to divine guidance to assist you with navigating change, you will see that there is a much bigger plan in store for you. There are always larger forces at work on your behalf. Change is meant to teach you this truth."

"The meeting of two personalities is like the contact of two chemical substances: if there is any reaction, both are transformed."

—Carl Gustav Jung

♥

"What is a teacher? I'll tell you: it isn't someone who teaches something, but someone who inspires the student to give of her best in order to discover what she already knows."

—Paulo Coelho, *The Witch of Portobello*

Chapter Six

Human Guidance Is Always Available

We all need steady, supportive, and insightful spiritual voices and perspectives—spiritual gravitational forces that ground us amidst our humanity. Sometimes our own spiritual perspective, bolstered and informed by our own practice, is enough. Other times, it's not, and we need more support. Throughout our lives, with variable frequency, we all need to access the support, guidance, facilitation, and wisdom that exists outside of ourselves, within the human beings walking amongst us.

That's by design—grand, divine design.

We are here to help each other; to teach, inspire, provoke, hold space for, nurture, walk with, and rise again. At our core, we are relational, and we're wired to find the

Souls meant to activate us, in whatever way, throughout our lifetimes. We each are meant to seek and find higher wisdom and assistance along our evolutionary paths. We're meant to reach for more and to find that more, at times, with the help of other people.

Caroline Myss calls it Spiritual Direction. Others, such as The Theosophical Society, wrote about the notion that when the student is ready, the teacher or the master appears—as if the appearance of wise spiritual teachers is a given within one's human lifetime. And it is.

It is a given that helpers will appear or arrive, in human form, to prompt, provoke, and accelerate your awakening.

Certainly, throughout history, we have deep traditions of spiritual teachers, gurus, or healers supporting and guiding other humans on their Soul journeys. Accompanying each other, on various legs of our journeys, is a tradition as old as time. Perhaps it's more than a tradition, though. Maybe it's a directive; that some teach, that some learn, that we all become changed, healed, and transformed within influential relationships. Perhaps that alchemical transformation is written into the blueprint of each of us. Perhaps all we have to do is accept it and participate.

There is deep, sacred value in the inclusion of outside, objective, observational people on your Soul journey. There is wisdom in knowing you can't do this alone, and most importantly, *that you aren't meant to.*

The Intrinsic Value of Building Your Spiritual Scaffolding

You are meant to gather reinforcements, recruit wise ones, and experience what others have to offer, all in the name of building your spiritual scaffolding. This structure wants to be established firmly and faithfully within your life, so you have the support, guidance, validation, processing, wisdom, and kindness you need on your journey of personal growth.

Build this structure, so you have ready access to love, hope, reassurance, and comradery. Create this so you have places where it's exquisitely safe to go deep, facing big truths that alter your life and soothe long-held wounds. Create your spiritual support structure, so you have access to beacons of light, pipelines to new ideas and wisdom, and portals to transformation. Build it, so it's there when you need it. Build it, faithfully aware that what arrives within this structure is meant to be.

Your Soul journey asks you to find the humans who activate and change you. Find their practices, teachings, books, workshops, retreats, one-on-one healing sessions, safe spaces, cozy offices, healing tables, music, art, writing, vibrations, frequencies, approaches, philosophies, wisdom, reminders, and gifts. Find those who are meant to contribute to your Soul journey and be open to receiving.

The act of building your earthly support structure is an act of self-care. It affirms that you are a priority; that you are valued, important, worth understanding, worth healing, and worth investment.

When you love yourself enough to reach for a witness, dedicated accompaniment, and a healing process, you're automatically opening yourself up to receive what you are seeking.

When you make yourself reachable, your Spirit Guides and loved ones on the Other Side will happily rise to meet you. They'll come through your teachers and healers and supportive helpers to give you what you need. When you take a step, in your human life, toward self-care, the Universe and all of its divine forces meet you there.

It's through relationships that we become more conscious. Within relationships, we grow, understand, gain clarity, and learn. Human relationships are a fundamental part of our journey. They propel us down the path of self-discovery because in knowing and experiencing others and what they bring us, we come to know ourselves.

> *Relationships, of all kinds, are gifts from the Universe and tools of the Soul.*

While not all relationships offer intimacy, and even more importantly, safe and sacred intimacy, we are wired to seek those that do. Many of us move through life experientially learning which relationships are best for us, coming to release those that aren't and cherishing those that are.

At our core, we want to share ourselves and our experiences, in safe and sacred ways, and build intimacy (whether physical, emotional, intellectual, or spiritual). We long to explore and understand our vulnerability with like-minded others because doing so allows us to deeply know ourselves. We know, intuitively, that relationships change us and, one way or another, spur us to become more conscious and aware.

In being seen, honored, and understood, we powerfully come to see, honor, and understand ourselves. Once that has occurred—once you know yourself in a new

IGNITE YOUR INTREPID SOUL

way—you never lose that. The truths that arise out of sacred, spiritual, and supportive relationships are powerful and lifelong. The shifts and the personal revelations that come with them never expire.

Building your spiritual scaffolding is a vital part of the Soul journey. It's a reflection of the value you place on yourself and your well-being. It's an act of personal responsibility and wisdom, and it exhibits a willingness to put into practice your deep-seated awareness that the journey toward your Soul is your life's path.

Creating the structure in your life that supports you on your journey thrills your Spirit Team; they enthusiastically guide and interact with you via this foundation of support. Granting yourself the gift of spiritual relationships, sacred support, and inspired change is inherently and remarkably self-loving. And, when you act from a place of self-love, you can transform anything.

Guiding Principles for Building Your Spiritual Scaffolding

So who do you put on this human team of yours? How do you find these right, sacred people to staff your spiritual scaffolding with their wisdom, guidance, and insight? There are a lot of people hanging their shingles, purporting to heal and help—which ones are right for you?

Good questions! Let's look at some guiding principles.

Who to Include on Your Human Team

We all resonate with different people, personality styles, practices, approaches, and philosophical perspectives. There is no "perfect" team that works for everyone, and so yours needs to be highly personalized.

To get you thinking creatively and openly, here's a shortlist of the kind of folks you might consider for your support team:

- Counselor

- Life Coach

- Acupuncturist

- Reiki Practitioner

- Shaman

- Energy or Body Worker

- Massage Therapist

- Intuitive Healer

- Psychic

- Medium

- Chiropractor

- Traditional Doctor

- Naturopathic Doctor

- Herbalist

- Plant Medicine Practitioner

- Flower Essence Practitioner

- Spiritual Travel/Trip Leader

- Past Life Regression Practitioner

- Crystal/Stone Practitioner

- Tarot Reader

- Trauma Specialists

- Sound/Frequency Healer

- Drum Journeyer

- Musician

- Creative Writing Coach

- Astrologer

- Art Teacher

- Religious Leader

- Conscious Relationship Teacher

One of the essential advantages of having a human team is this: it's an intimate, safe structure that you can step into when something comes up. We all need guidance and accompaniment. There are times you'll know exactly what's coming up or going on or causing a problem in your world. Other times, you simply need to show up in a safe, trusted place, throwing up your hands in confusion or exhaustion, knowing that the person in front of you will help you return to your center or create order amidst the chaos.

As you know, your human experiences inform and teach you—sometimes, you need another set of eyes and ears to help translate what life is showing you.

When the pain, intensity, and provocation of the human experiences hits, you need a place where healing is invited, facilitated, and of primary focus—a place where you can take the time and space you need to restore the pathways to your Soul.

Meanwhile, there are times when life feels a-okay, and you'll just want to check in, perhaps to take in some Soul maintenance. You don't need to be in crisis to engage with your spiritual support team! In fact, the most powerful healing sessions and conversations can come when the agenda isn't urgent or acute, and there's room to engage, wander, explore, and consider.

Your Soul invites you to find those people, who, at the right time and in the right way, act as gentle questioners and observers; those who offer guidance and accompaniment into the depths of your Soul; the ones who journey alongside you, holding space for healing, curiosity, emotion, questioning, and truth. If you're open to finding them, your Soul will help make them available to you.

Discernment and Choice in Building Your Spiritual Scaffolding

As is the case with your intuition and spirit guidance, discernment has a role in this process. In fact, discernment should *govern* this process. Remember: you know the truth by the way it feels. And, particularly, you know, deep within yourself, who feels right for you and who does not.

You know those "vibes" you get about other people? Those hunches or senses? The cautionary energy or the intense draw? When you just know, without words or explanation, who is right and who is not? This is discernment. Trust it. Use it, unabashedly, in this process of building your spiritual scaffolding.

To get you centered and grounded in this task, consider these questions:

- What environments feel most safe for you? What kind of people feel most safe for you?

- Who does your Soul want to bring into your life? What kind of learning or wisdom is your Soul seeking at this time?

- What have you always been drawn to or been curious about trying in terms of healing experiences?

- What messages have you received recently, intuitively or otherwise, indicating to what or to whom you're being guided?

- When you consider expressing your vulnerability or looking deep within yourself, what kind of person or environment feels most safe? Most helpful?

- What unlocks your creativity? Your emotions? What makes you feel, cry, or emote?

- What activities did you love to do as a child? What made you feel happy, blissful, or carefree as a child?

- What do you long to do? When you say, *"If I didn't have to work,"* or *"I had more money,"*...how do you finish that sentence?

- When you review the list of sample practitioners offered earlier, who/what stands out to you?

Consider your initial, knee-jerk responses to these questions. For instance, if deep one-on-one conversation unlocks your emotions and prompts you to open up, move toward a person who offers that intimate relational experience. Or, if you realize that if you didn't have to work, you'd sign on for a pilgrimage to a sacred site, take note of this and consider that traveling, especially spiritual traveling, is likely a worthwhile endeavor for you.

Notice what you long for. Do you long for rest? Conversation? Do you long to be heard and seen? Do you long for music or art or permission to be creative? To travel or to experience the freedom of exploration? Do you long to visit a particular country, place, or culture? Have you always been drawn to crystals, plant medicine, or natural remedies? Do you long for a place where you can learn about these things and ask questions freely?

Please notice these longings. Please give them weight, value, and consideration. Don't ignore your intuitive hits, nagging hunches, or deep longings; these are directional signs on your journey.

> *Your Soul is leaving you an intuitive breadcrumb trail that leads you to the humans whose gifts you're meant to receive.*

When you center into your intuition with the intention of building your spiritual scaffolding, you'll find that discernment comes quickly and clearly. You'll simply *know* what to try, who to consider, and where to step. Pair these insights with action: make that phone call, book the appointment, begin the process.

Your Soul wants you to discover the transformational human relationships that await you. They're orchestrated from afar, divinely chosen and directed on your behalf.

When Your Spirit Guides Weigh In

Your Spirit Guides and loved ones on the Other Side will be active in this process too. They might leave you affirming signs or signals: finding a penny in the parking lot of your new counselor's office, seeing a cardinal fly through your backyard during a phone call with your coach, or receiving an invitation from a friend to join a tai chi class for trauma survivors.

In fact, one of the ways your loved ones on the Other Side and your Spirit Guides assist is by directly sending you the human guides, facilitators, healers, and accompaniment you need on your journey.

Some of these people might be familiar to you (and to your Soul!), while others might be new to you. Some might offer tried-and-true healing methods you know well, while others might bring something brand-new—something that challenges or stretches you—to your world.

Some might have unique, exquisite access to your guides and Higher Self, while others might be sacred listeners and offer the kind of feedback that helps you order your emotional world and unlock deep insights.

Trust who comes to you and who comes across your path. Trust your inklings, longings, and curiosities. Trust when a friend invites you to a refreshing new healing experience. Trust your dreams and visions. Trust that the healer your aunt has been raving about for years might be worth a try. Trust it if suddenly, in your social media feed, you see advertisements for specific healing modalities.

When it comes to getting your attention, your Spirit Guides and loved ones on the Other Side aren't subtle—they want you to heal, evolve, and transform.

A Message from the Other Side

"You are not alone. We have sent the wisdom, leadership, assistance, and information you need, in the form of other humans and their teachings. We have sent you our divine proxies. Find them. Embrace them. Let yourself be changed and healed by your engagements with them."

How to Build Your Team

As you begin to build your spiritual scaffolding or add to what you already have in place, it's helpful to draw your attention inward, checking in with your own center of truth.

Consider your own values and the values you would like to find in teachers, supporters, or spiritual facilitators. For instance, you might require:

- Someone who has firm and healthy boundaries, and makes their boundaries clear and up-front in their work.

- Someone who values and stands by confidentiality and trust.

- Someone who understands the value of creating a safe, supported space, and the responsibility to safe-guard that intimate space.

- Someone who listens, honors, and seeks to validate your life experiences.

- Someone who challenges or pushes you, in the right way, to look at things differently or to stretch or grow.

- Someone who values honesty and speaks up, even when it's difficult.

- Someone who offers alternative points of view or prompts questioning or curiosity.

You are looking for the people, practices, and expe-riences that are going to bring you closer to your Soul. Consider what you need to feel, know, and trust to safely step into that process.

Consider your own comfort level: gender, location, per-sonality style, office space, approach—if you feel strongly about any of these, note that in your search process.

It's okay to begin with what feels most comforting to you. You can't heal if you don't feel safe.

In addition to trusting where your intuition and discernment lead you, consider the modern approach: The Google Search.

Or, for our purposes, *The Sacredly Intentioned Google Search.*

Here's how it works:

- When you're ready to find your next teacher, healer, or wise helper, set an intention. For instance, *I am prepared to receive guidance regarding the best person to help me on my spiritual path and healing journey.*

- Search for what you're looking for: *spiritual healers in my area* or *sound frequency healers* or *transformative life coach* or *meditation therapists*. As you do this, hold your intention within your body. Sit grounded with your feet on the floor. Sit up tall and breathe freely, feeling your center opening and ready to receive.

- Trust where you're drawn: a particular website, a series of headshots and bios, a pathway of clicks that lead you four pages away to someone's blog. And, for instance, if presented with a series of headshots, *feel* who is best for you. Scan that lineup and feel for that best fit. Or, if you're reading through bios or philosophical approaches, note what resonates with you and what tugs at you.

- Remember: pair whatever presents itself with your intuition and discernment. Check what you receive against your gut. *Feel if it's right.*

Your intuition and discernment are vital tools. The process of healing is highly experiential, and so you need to be in it, feeling it, to know what's right for you.

Also, it's okay to give someone a try and back up if it's not the right fit. You may not find an exact match on the first try; it may take a few passes at building your support structure until you have your ideal combination of helpers assembled. Trust the process even when it takes longer than you anticipated; sometimes learning what doesn't work for you is profoundly enlightening and valuable.

Be curious and intuitive about this process and trust what you feel.

Remember the Value of Conversation

We are meant to process our experiences and the emotional content that arises out of those experiences. Since we are inherently relational beings, there is intrinsic value in sharing our stories with each other. We often feel better when we unburden ourselves by giving voice to our experiences. The value of sharing is magnified when our stories and experiences are honored—when another person, or group of people, listens, receives, and validates what we've shared.

That experience of being honored arises from the safety present within real intimacy. For instance, you've surely experienced sharing something with someone who just didn't listen, care, or respond. Undoubtedly, you felt the stalling of the conversational process, and you might have withdrawn, stopped sharing, or conversely, perhaps you continued to share in hopes you could make the other person see or understand your experience. Either way, the conversation fell out of balance, and you probably came away feeling worse than when it began. We've all had these experiences, and the truth is that they just don't feel good, and they're certainly not representative of safe, honoring intimacy.

On the other hand, you likely have experienced being heard—*really heard*—when another person engages with you, through body language, eye contact, demonstrated support and response, insightful feedback, or supportive follow-up questions. You know this experience because you feel listened to, received, and validated. You know this kind of safe intimacy wherein conversation, sharing, and vulnerability are welcomed and secure. Within this conversational space, what's shared transforms, becoming something you can work with: a healing, an insight, a weight lifted, increased self-awareness, the release of heaviness, or the sense that puzzle pieces have finally fallen into place.

When you share a tender part of yourself, and it is honored, you've set free something that had previously been embedded within you. This is a shift into a more conscious and aware space where hope, action, and transformation can take root and grow.

> *When you tell your truth, secrets lose their power; when you voice honesty, anything less than it falls away.*

Meanwhile, the other profound gift of conversation is that of thoughtful, wise, or perspective-shifting feedback. You don't know what you don't know. You can only see as far as you've expanded. And that's okay; that's entirely expected!

Sometimes we underestimate or forget the value of simply receiving feedback or having our assumptions questioned. Sometimes the input itself is revelatory and unlocks a deep place of clarity, truth, or healing. Sometimes, the value of feedback is simply in the process of talking something through, processing out loud, being heard, or reacting to another viewpoint.

The conversational back-and-forth is reflective of the relational nature of our Souls. We are wired to bounce off of each other, prompting each other to respond, shift, grow, and be changed. Sometimes, it's the process of bouncing that does the trick, and other times, the value is in what we receive within the exchange.

"Shame dies when stories are told in safe spaces."

—Amy Voskamp

Ultimately, we are here, on this planet, in human form, to be changed. It's hard to deny that the right conversation, with the right person or group of people, at the right time, is a powerful catalyst for transformation.

Remember this when building your spiritual scaffolding: *the sacred power of conversation and sharing is an echo of the divine, relational nature of our Souls.*

A Message from the Other Side

"The feeling and experience of belonging is powerful for you, both as a Soul and as a human being. One of your most sacred means of connecting to each other and feeling that deep sense of belonging is through the act of storytelling and listening. This exchange of experience and understanding builds relationships, comradery, and fosters a sense of belonging. Remember, you always belong: to the Universe, to your Soul, to the heartbeat of evolution, to each other. Sharing yourself with others will remind you of that and bring you great comfort."

The Courageous Act of Letting Someone In

It takes tremendous courage to engage in self-discovery and healing. It takes even more courage to let someone into that space with you. And while the outcomes are often evolutionary and life-changing, sometimes it feels as if it takes everything you have simply to reach out and start.

If this is the case for you, know this: *You are not alone.* And, you deserve to experience what comes on the other side of this fear and anxiety.

So many of us come from backgrounds that work against the divine urging to build trusting, sincere, healing relationships. Such scenarios might include:

- If you come from a family system or religious tradition that requires secret-keeping and disallows truth-telling that could undermine the family or organization.

- If you have a trauma history that may have left you conditioned to keep your experiences and stories hidden and even secret.

- If your gender conditioning is such that you received messages that feeling and expressing emotion and pain is weak or shameful.

- If in your childhood or throughout your life it wasn't safe to trust other people or you've been endangered, abused, or neglected within intimate relationships.

- If you come from a background in which talking, expressing, and feeling weren't welcomed or even discouraged, and therefore, you never learned or experienced what it was like to safely express yourself.

- If you are deeply fearful that looking at or processing old trauma or wounding will destabilize you or
  your life.

If any of these points—or others like them—resonate
with you, it's important to honor that allowing another
person into your depths may feel daunting, scary, uncomfortable, and even triggering. You've probably felt,
throughout your life, that it isn't safe to be vulnerable
with someone in that way, and doubtful that your experiences could be understood or helped. You might have
deep-seated fears of rejection, ridicule, shame, or humili-
ation. It's important to know that these fears might come
up as you consider reaching out to invite someone onto
your spiritual support team.

Honor this truth for yourself. Your fears are normal
and allowed; if you don't know what a trusting relationship looks like, you're allowed to feel daunted and anxious. Please breathe, honor, and love yourself through
these triggers.

As best you can, lean on these divine truths: Helpers
will always be available to you when you ask for them.
Your Soul and your Spirit Guides haven't left you here,
abandoned, and without support. There are people on the
planet who are suited—precisely suited—to you. There are
people whose expertise is just what you need. There are
people whose style, approach, and tone are custom-craft-

ed for you. Those who would act as loving change agents in your life are walking among you.

> *"Somehow we've come to equate success with not needing anyone. Many of us are willing to extend a helping hand, but we're very reluctant to reach out for help when we need it ourselves. It's as if we've divided the world into "those who offer help" and "those who need help." The truth is that we are both."*
>
> —Brené Brown

Truly, for so many of us, it's an act of courage, even defiance, to say *"no more"* and decide to heal. It's brave to bring in a team of supportive people because it reflects the stopping of old cycles, breaking of generational patterns, and consciously undoing conditioned belief systems. Sometimes, it's hard to believe that you aren't alone, and you're going to have to leap in faith to get to the other side of that terrifying precipice.

If it feels like a big deal—to decide to heal and to begin to build your team of spiritual, supportive wisdom-bring-ers—you're right. It is. But you're here for big.

You're here to confront the human illusions that keep you from your Soul. You're here to reclaim *you*, relieving suffering and finding fullness and joy. You are here to accept the invitation to rise—above and beyond the experiences impacting you—and step into a supported, conscious, and loved life. These aren't lofty goals; they're the goals of your Soul. Find the helpers your Soul has sent for you.

 ## SACRED INTENTION-SETTING:
Who Is Meant to Be Part of Your Spiritual Scaffolding

For this intention, return to your Soul Fire. Settle in someplace comfortable and close your eyes and imagine returning to your Soul Fire. Sit next to its warmth and comfort. Let its power guide you at this moment.

When you're ready, read silently or aloud this intention:

I welcome the comfort and companionship offered by my Soul Fire. I soak in its warmth, I feel its support, and I welcome its truth. I ask that my Soul Fire give me insight and guidance as I seek to build my spiritual scaffolding. I ask for indications of the kinds of people or practitioners who are ideal for me at this time. I ask for insight into the style, characteristics, and feel of the people who are in my Highest and Best Honor at this time. I welcome knowing where to begin, who to reach out to, where to explore, and how to receive. I welcome intuitive clues along the way; I will pay attention to these clues and respond accordingly. I welcome any resistance I have to this process to come to the surface, where I can honor it and hear it out. I also welcome the focus and knowledge of my Soul to keep me clear and grounded as I move with and through any fears or resistance.

POWERING INTENTION WITH ACTION

What action step or two can you take coming out of that intention process? What phone call can you make? What website can you consult? Is there a trusted family member, friend, or colleague from whom you might seek a referral? What fear or block can you honor and lovingly step through? How can you honor your next right step toward building your spiritual scaffolding?

Managing the Team Roster

Your spiritual scaffolding is yours to build, dismantle, rebuild, adjust, maintain, and evaluate. Add and subtract to and from your team as needed. Audit your team with regularity.

Someone will rarely journey with you for your entire life. It's far more common that, per the Universe, people are in your life for specific seasons, bringing you interaction and engagement, provoking thought or action, or offering new paradigms or wisdom when you most need them, at the times you're most ready for them.

This harkens back to the Theosophical Society's notion that the teacher arrives when the student is ready. Someone might arrive on your scene, and your job will be to welcome that teacher. Or, the time of journeying with a teacher, guide, or healer will come to a natural end, and you'll need to note this and release or adjust.

Check in with yourself from time to time, to keep your human team robust, helpful, and useful.

To do this, you might ask yourself:

- Who feels safe and supportive? Is there anyone who no longer feels this way?

- What wise gifts does this person bring to me when we have a conversation or a healing session? Is there anyone who no longer offers those gifts? Is there someone whose gifts I've received, fulfilling and completing the purpose of the relationship?

- Is there anyone who has made their mark and from whom I am ready to move on? Is there anyone with whom I need more or less contact?

- Is there a teacher or healer I especially like with whom I might engage more deeply?

You can also decide what pace and frequency feel right for you. There might be a time in your life when you're experiencing a significant crisis and need all hands on deck. At these times, it might be essential to have weekly appointments on the books, so you're stepping into a safe, supportive, healing space with regularity. Other times, you might take a deep, extended dive with a specific teacher, counselor, or healer, and find that the intensive one-on-one process feels right, authentic, and expansive.

There is, of course, no pressure to engage with all members of your spiritual team at one time. Most of us can't do that, given time, financial resources, and emotional bandwidth—and that's okay! Don't overload yourself. The key is deftness: choosing the people and places that are right for you at the right time on your journey, and having the courage and commitment to step into those healing conversations or sessions when you need them.

Some Final Thoughts

Consider your resources, but don't use them as an excuse not to begin or receive. Many people will immediately say, *"I can't afford that!"* or *"I don't have time for that!"* As humans, we love a good fear-based "reason" to not step into change, or the unknown, or the discomfort of our depths.

> *Please don't let your fears or discomfort turn into excuses that stunt your growth.*

There will always—always—be an excuse. There will always be not enough money or not enough time. There will always be a reason to not start or change or leap. Trust your resources and yourself, and place value on the process of healing and aligning with your Soul.

Also, remain open to compelling single experiences—the ones that prompt instant change. Help will always present itself to those who ask for it, and our Souls and Spirit Guides work in serendipitous, mystical ways to deploy Universal forces on our behalf.

Sometimes, you might connect with a powerful message or experience in a single encounter: at a workshop or a class; at lunch with a best friend; in a conversation with an elder; at the book signing of a spiritual author.

Sometimes, the gift of awakening comes in a single moment—a flash—and you're changed, instantly. In those cases, it will have been vital to trust your intuition and accept the lunch invitation or the nudge to attend the workshop. When you're trusting of and responding to your intuitive nudges, you're more easily placed in the right place at the right time.

> *Awakening so often arrives in serendipitous, like-a-ton-of-bricks moments. Go where you're guided. Respond to those nudges. The Universe is constantly conspiring to bring you face-to-face with those moments.*

Allow your Soul to lead you to experiences with other people. Follow the leads that feel right and remain open to hearing, seeing, or receiving what's meant for you.

A Message from the Other Side

"You have come to Earth with a contingent of like-minded Souls. Some will be your teachers, some will be your healers, some will facilitate for you, some will hold you in nourishing love. You are never far from fellow humans equipped and able to advance your Soul journey. Look for them, attune your vibration to them, welcome them into your life. They bring life-giving resources to you, in both dark and light times. Allow this assistance, for it is sacred."

"Fate is how your life unfolds when you let fear determine your choices. A path of destiny reveals itself to you, however, when you confront your fear and make conscious choices."

—Caroline Myss

--- ♥ ---

"The path isn't a straight line, it's a spiral. You continually come back to things you thought you understood and see deeper truths."

—Barry H. Gillespie

Chapter Seven

The Unstoppable Force of Awakening

O nce you start your own healing process, you cannot
stop. You can take breaks and rests, but you cannot
stop. Awakening, once it's begun, consistently reveals the
Universe's secrets and their connection to you.

When you have glimpsed your life through the eyes
of spirit—when you've understood, even for a moment,
that your human life is a sacred, spiritual endeavor—you
have reached an existential point of no return. You aren't
the same and won't ever be the same again. And the only
direction to go from here is *onward*.

It's a triumph that you're here. You've arrived in
this place where you've immersed yourself, willingly, in
the current of your Soul (though not without moments

of reservation, resistance, or fear). You look like and act like someone who knows there is something much larger—more mystical and more divine—at work in your human life.

You've done such important work to arrive here:

- You have discovered and heard the beautiful sound of your intuition, and now you know just how spot-on it is. You're inspired and able to integrate your intuition into your life with devoted commitment.

- You have opened to the truth of spiritual guidance and grown closer to your loved ones on the Other Side and your Spirit Guides. These friendly and loving forces accompany you as you navigate life from this point forward.

- You have embraced personal responsibility. You are becoming curious about knowing, understanding, and valuing yourself in unprecedented ways, aware that loving and taking responsible care of yourself is the greatest gift you can give to the world.

- You have built a team of supportive resources that provide you with inspiration, healing, and processing whenever you need assistance.

- And finally, you have made and are continuing to make changes, small and large, taking single right steps and occasional big leaps, and recognizing the fear that comes up as part of the evolutionary process.

If you're doing parts of this, all of this, or something in between, you're living spiritually. You're living in congruence with your Soul. That you're here is beautiful, wonderful, and triumphant!

And now: keep going.

Give yourself over to the true nature of healing and awakening. Don't fight it when something else comes up for you to look at, don't resist new inconvenient truths, and don't be dismayed when you revisit a wound you thought you'd already healed.

The path of healing and evolution isn't linear; it's circular. In walking the Soul path, you won't walk in a straight line; instead, you'll walk in a sacred circle.

You'll discover new truths and keep revisiting those truths even when they aren't new anymore. You'll return, again and again, to wounds, patterns, habits, and old spots that tripped you up—not because you failed or missed something, but because there is more for you to learn. The layers peel back, revealing depth, nuance, and even more truth. There's more unfolding—there's more here, *for you*—on the circular path of healing.

Don't mistake the evolutionary nature of the Soul journey for some failing on your part. Don't mistake the constant returning and exploring, the ebb and the flow, for something you've done wrong. You aren't stuck or regressed or back at square one. No, you are on the loop of awakening, ready at each juncture to learn something new or to evolve just a bit more.

This way of life won't quit, and it asks you, over and over again, to keep looking with curiosity, willingness, and faith. Each turn and decision point asks you to go deeper into your sacred center. Living in alignment with your Soul rewrites your entire human operation, requiring process, evolution, refinement, and the continuous revealing of truth. If you can stay with this perennial movement and resist taking it personally, you'll continue to receive magnificent, transformative, and clarifying gifts—gifts that are your birthright.

A Message from the Other Side

"Nothing dies, and nothing ends. Energy simply changes shape and form, constantly breathing, in and out. Such is your Soul's path. Your journey of evolution does not end; rather, it returns, bringing you deeper and closer to truth and wholeness. The human mind thinks in linear ways while the Soul knows of the ever-deepening journey inward."

When Your Soul Asks for Another Deep Dive

Awakening creates a space for reflection. We are often proud of our journeys, as we should be, and feel confident and good about how far we've come. It's essential to take in the hard work completed, the time and energy invested, the emotions processed, the dark nights lived through, the confusion resolved. This place feels satisfying. It's tempting to consider the journey done.

While you're proud of how far you've come, you aren't necessarily excited about doing something like it again. When you've come through this kind of awakening, you know what it takes and just how low the lows can feel. Of course, the highs make it worth it. But, it can still feel daunting to think that, someday, you might get the call to go back in, to take another deep dive.

The truth is that the call will come again. You *will* be called to step back in, to encounter more darkness and confusion, or comb through complex emotional content. It's the nature of life. It's the truth of the Soul.

At this moment, at this next crossroads, it's crucially important to remember: you haven't regressed, or strayed from the path, or fallen down, or lost ground. When you are at this familiar place where the Soul beckons you to go deep once again, it's going to be very easy to worry, even panic, that somehow, you've gone off-path. Or messed up. Or are lost. That's how the human brain works: here you are, at another profound challenge, and you *must* have done something to cause this—something about you *must* be wrong or broken. But you haven't done anything wrong, and you are not broken. You are simply human.

This is a powerful place where so many of us fall victim to the ego's misrepresentation that we've somehow failed. You begin to doubt the work you've done or are hard on yourself for losing your way after "*all that work.*" It's vitally important that you reframe this mindset. It's vitally important that you not take this personally.

You see, you aren't back where you started or stuck or off-path.

When you do the work of your Soul, healing yourself and discovering life-changing truths, those transformations don't expire. They're permanent.

The caterpillar that went into that cocoon and came out the butterfly? It's never a caterpillar again. And you aren't who you were when you began this journey.

It's entirely reasonable that when you face another call to go deep and work on a piece of healing, some of your old patterns will come up. What you need to remember is that these patterns, habits, choices, narratives, fears, or anxieties aren't indications that you've somehow fallen back to ground zero—no! It's normal and completely okay that these things have arisen again. These are signals that you simply need to take another pass at learning, healing, shifting, and understanding them.

Throughout our lives, we return to places we know well so that we can go deeper, learn more, and gather new insights. There are always more gifts to collect from our human experiences as we become ready to see new themes, take more responsibility, or more powerfully understand old patterns. The layers and nuances of what we've previously processed offer more clues and insights that help us further unlock our vibrance and truth.

You have arrived at this crossroads of next steps because it's time—and you are ready—for another layer of healing, another series of self-discoveries, and another step in your evolution. This is by design, and you couldn't stop it, even if you tried. This place isn't a punishment or an indication that you've gone wrong. In fact, this place is an indication that you're doing just what you should be doing: walking, with responsibility and curiosity, on your Soul path, taking up what's before you as it comes. This place is an indication that you're right where you belong and that you're ready for more evolution, growth, truth, and Soul alignment.

That your Soul is tapping your shoulder, nudging you down another path of self-discovery is a sign that you're ready for more. You're ready to evolve, grow, transform, and awaken—a little bit more.

It's okay to arrive here with a sigh of wariness or an anxious sense of anticipation. That is the spiritual journey, isn't it? You know you're about to feel a bunch of emotions, challenge a host of old patterns, and face some inconvenient truths. You don't need to throw a party in celebration, and it's okay to feel trepidation about what's ahead of you, but don't avoid it. Walk forward. Take that next right step.

When you can recognize that you're at the precipice of another deep, self-reflective leg of your journey, reframe your negative self-talk, and step into what's ahead, knowing you're working *with* the forces of life.

This place of invitation and action builds self-trust, and that's why reframing the negative self-talk is so important: without doing so, you miss an opportunity to trust yourself to accept life's invitation to keep growing.

When you acknowledge that life is a series of invitations to awaken, and you're able to accept those invitations and trust the spiritual process, you build magnificent self-trust and congruence with your Soul.

When you can heed the call of your Soul to do another round of healing work, you're moving into a space of true mastery of the human experience.

Know this: if it's time for more healing, it's because you're ready, you're prepared, and *you can do thi*s.

SACRED INTENTION-SETTING:
Discovering the Next Step on Your Soul Journey

As we move into this intention, consider whether it's time for you to embark upon the next leg of your healing journey. If it is and you're ready for another deep dive—or even just a moderate dive—then settle into this intention. Feel your supported center and the deep knowledge that your Soul and the Universe will always reveal the truth to you when you ask for it. Imagine sitting next to your Soul Fire, open and curious, nourished and loved.

When you're ready, read silently or aloud this intention:

I welcome the support, guidance, insight, and loving kindness of my Soul Fire, my Spirit Guides, and the Universe. As I settle here, I open with curiosity to consider what lies before me on my personal healing journey. What truth am I meant to awaken to next? What pattern, situation, or belief is at play in my life that offers insight into the next piece of healing work before me? What is my next deep dive? If I choose to step into this process of healing, repairing, and awakening, what will I gain? What will I release? How will my life be lifted or improved if I step into this next place of awakening? What supportive action might I take as a first step toward this end?

**POWERING INTENTION
WITH ACTION**

What next truth was revealed to you within that intention-setting process? Are you ready to name that truth or follow that next path of healing? If so, what does that piece of work need to be supported and successful? Is there someone on your human support team you need to contact? Do you need to find a new practitioner or coach? How might you prepare to take a few right steps to begin this next leg of your Soul journey? What do you need to remember and take in as nourishment as you do so?

Action Is the Change Agent of Your Soul

As someone committed to the journey of the Soul and the ebb and flow of healing, you'll discover that you must begin to build a life that is congruent with your Soul—a life that reflects what you've learned and how you've changed. It creates more suffering to *not* live like you're changed.

If you've done some healing work and come up with some essential truths, but you haven't worked those insights into your life, this where you can start to feel "stuck." This in-between is a classic place where frustration, fatigue, anxiety, even panic or fear set in. You tell yourself you shouldn't feel this way, that you've done so much work, and life shouldn't be so hard. And you're not far off base! The key, however, is action. And that shouldn't come as a surprise—you know this. *Action is the change agent of the Soul.*

When you're in the space between ah-ha and not-quite-living-it-yet, the cure for what ails you is action.

This feeling, masquerading as "stuck," is actually an urging to take steps toward making your life more congruent with what you've learned. Your inner world wants to be translated into your outer world. This space seeks to be where you transform: where you retire what no longer works for you, start making new choices, break old patterns, choose more consciously, and step toward healthy self-love. Here, your Soul is demanding that you live in more intentioned congruence with what you've learned.

You wouldn't be able to access these places of profound insight if you weren't capable of taking the corresponding action, even when it's hard to do so.

The Soul path consistently asks you to self-actualize—that is, to take conscious action to integrate the wisdom, uniqueness, and the divine signature of your Soul into your human life.

The path of the Soul requires you to take what you've learned, at each juncture, and carry it forward into your life. The Soul asks you to put into practice what you've clarified, making new choices based on the ah-ha moments you've collected and taking faithful action born out of what you now know is right for you.

A Message from the Other Side

"You exist in human form, in a physical body, on the planet Earth so that you may engage with action. As a human, you feel and experience the energy of action as it swells up inside of you, emerges, and then leaves you, whether intentioned or not, creating your reality. We encourage you to more deeply understand that action creates your reality, and ask you to be aware of the places from which you act and create."

The New You:
Integrating Your Soul into Your Life

So here you are: the place where you know too much truth about yourself to ever, ever, return to where you came from, but perhaps not quite enough to know what's next. You can't go back, but you're not entirely clear on how to move forward.

Much the way intuition and spirit guidance require you to pair them with action to realize their self-empowering benefits, living with your Soul is going to require its own version of powerful and clarifying action: *integration*.

Integrative action is how you take concepts, insights, new ideas, lessons learned, healthy narratives, and fresh perspectives and sew them into the fabric of your life, anchoring your healing work, and creating real-life transformation.

Integration creates congruence between your inner and outer world, making your human self more reflective of your Soul. As you integrate these transformations in your life, you'll need to act, speak, choose, engage, think, interpret, and *be* in accordance with the deeply held truths of your Soul.

You can be preemptive about this change, taking a piece of healing work you've done, and bringing it directly to the areas of your life where you know it can make a clarifying or favorable impact.

Alternatively, you might not entirely be aware of all the change required, or you might be mindful of the necessary change, but it's daunting, and you've put it off. Like small areas of irritation or wounds that want soothing, you'll soon begin to notice where in your life you need to adjust. As you know, your human experience will show you where to focus your attention and healing efforts.

To make this clearer, let's look at two examples where work might be needed: relationships and fulfillment.

PRUNING RELATIONSHIPS

Because we are relational beings and learn so many of our lessons within relationships, this is an area that frequently requires attention, clearing, action, and integration. If there's an old pattern at work or an unhealthy narrative playing out, your relationships will reveal those to you. Relationships are our truth tellers.

Symptoms:

- You find that some of your relationships aren't as rewarding or fulfilling as they used to be, or that you don't want to spend time with the people you used to spend time with in the past.

- You recognize that an old pattern you've been working to heal is in play in your relationship with your partner, and while you're anxious about putting a stop to it, you know you can no longer abide by the status quo.

- You realize that conversations aren't deep enough, or connections aren't intimate or safe enough with a group of friends you've traditionally sought out.

- You realize that spending time alone is more rejuvenating than spending time with other people.

Integrative Action:

These symptoms are a classic point of tension, particularly after you've worked through old relationship patterns, wounds, or narratives. You see, when you shift yourself, you no longer need to draw in the same kinds of relationships to help you notice, recognize, and heal what's been unconscious. We often unconsciously pull in the people who teach us what we need to learn, and some of them, ultimately, have to go when we've learned the lesson.

Sometimes, releasing a relationship is incredibly difficult, and other times, it will feel like ripping off a band-aid—surprisingly easy. Other times, the answer isn't necessarily to release a relationship; instead, it might require restructuring or new boundaries. You might need to bravely speak up about your expectations and the ways the relationship needs to change for you to remain in it. You might need to adjust the weight or value you place on the relationship or change your expectations of what it offers you.

Your relationships are one of the first areas to experience tension when you haven't quite yet integrated the lessons you've learned. Be brave about pruning that relationship tree—when you do, it makes room for the new and right relationships to enter your life.

REDEFINING FULFILLMENT

Like relationships, what's been part of your life is reflective of what you needed to learn, realize, understand, or heal to awaken and evolve. When you've done this—even a small part of it—you're energetically and vibrationally shifted, and so, what needed to play out around you no longer needs to do so. What you needed to witness to bring about the personal ah-ha moment or the pain point that drove you to engage in a healing process, is no longer necessary. And so, it must go.

Symptoms:

- You find yourself wanting something more, different, better, something more fulfilling, more aligned with your truth, more intimate, more real.

- You've realized you no longer need to suffer the way you have been or settle for something that doesn't honor, help, serve, or empower you, and you're ready for change.

- You're feeling irritable, frustrated, and restless in your life, and you're not sure where or how to begin to resolve those feelings.

- You crave or long for the feeling of breaking out of or shedding some old container or mindset.

Integrative Action:

These symptoms of longing and craving are fundamentally important. When you long for deeper connection, real intimacy, honesty and truth, fulfillment and joy, this is a sign that you're ready to move beyond the previous version of you and step into the new you. There's a reason what pleased, contented, or satisfied you before no longer does: you're different! When you know what doesn't work and you've healed the source of that imbalance, your entire being craves what *does* work.

Follow those longings and cravings. Be courageous in letting go of what no longer works for you and in pursuing what does work. Take steps to audit your life, remove the things that feel depleting or irritating, and replace them with what you *truly want*. Be aware that this can often include making changes that other people may dislike, and you might need to anchor and support yourself as you make some of these shifts.

One Step at a Time

While integrating what you've learned or healed in your life, don't mistake places of frustration, irritability, sadness, or stuckness for powerlessness. The illusion, of course, is that you're stuck and powerless to make a change or feel better, but the truth is the opposite.

This place of tension is calling for you to rise up and step into not only your power, but also self-trust, courage, self-love, and faith, in a brand-new way. This place prompts you to leap past the human fear that you're stuck and instead begin with diligence the job of making a series of right, conscious steps.

These small, step-by-step choices help you practically move forward while soothing your fearful mindset. For instance, if, as part of your recent healing process, you became aware and accepted that your marriage must end, it might be easy to get stuck here. This is a huge change that brings up any number of fears. It's "easy" to not begin the work of that change, to let your fears amplify, and to stay put. But, truth doesn't work that way. The Soul doesn't work that way.

If you've admitted it, that truth is a seed that will grow, sprout, and bloom. It'll come up through the crack in the concrete if it has to. If you ignore it, it'll cause you pain and suffering. It'll make itself more prominent and more blatant if you try to ignore it. However, if you are, even though you're fearful, able to implement this difficult and even grievous reality into your life one right step at a time, you'll be working *with* the energy of that growing, blooming truth. You'll be integrating something you deeply and profoundly know to be right into your human life.

This kind of integrative action, especially the type that requires you to rebirth yourself, revealing your deepest convictions, strengths, courage, and bravery, is what transforms you.

While the leaps, big and small, required to begin
making these corrective and sacred adjustments really test you, they offer sacred pivot points of alignment,
empowerment, and awakening. It's the integrative action
that heals. It cements the hard work you've done and provides a brand-new foundation of self-love, self-trust, fulfillment, vibrancy, and Soul alignment. Integrative action
takes bravery, and not everyone in your life will like it, but
it's worth all of the effort and conviction you put into it.

 ## SACRED INTENTION-SETTING:
Discovering Your Next Integrative Action

For this intention, return again to your Soul Fire. Sit be-
side it, taking in its warmth and support. Your Soul Fire is
particularly fond of action and will power any intention
you set or commitment you make here.

When you're ready, read silently or aloud this intention:

*I welcome the friendly, purifying, and empowering force of inte-
grative action. I open to its guidance and direction, welcoming
its conviction and determination to make my life more fulfilled,
authentic, and vibrant. I appreciate working with the integrative action and open to what it would like to reveal to me at
this moment. I am curious about what integrative action I could*

take, at this time, in my life, to live more congruently with my Soul. I ask for support, encouragement, bravery, and vision as I prepare to take integrative action. I commit to loving and honoring myself through this process, particularly when it's difficult or demands I face fear, loss, or challenge. I allow the reassuring energy of integrative action to fill my body, noting the way it supports me, loves me, and urges me bravely forward.

 POWERING INTENTION WITH ACTION

What integrative action appears in this process? How does that call to action make you feel? Before this process, were you aware of this integrative action, or is it new information? Do you feel confident about making these shifts or changes? Does this work daunt you? What can you do, right now, today, to support yourself in taking the action you know is necessary for your life? How might you remember and keep close the knowledge that integrative action will always be worth the effort?

The Forgiving Nature of Integrative Action

Sometimes, in facing the need to adjust or change, you lose sight of your way, and old narratives and limiting beliefs take over. Your fearful mind runs rampant with reasons not to change and rationalizations advocating the status quo. And then, perhaps just as quickly as you found yourself feeling stuck or lost, you regain your footing and know, in your whole being, what you must do. You're clear again, and though you're still afraid, you feel more resolute.

This ping-ponging is normal. It's natural. It's part of the process. And it takes practice. You'll find that living a spiritual life, aligned with your Soul and narrated by intuitive forces, gives you plenty of practice in navigating this space of knowing, forgetting, remembering, and leaping. You'll also find that the more you engage in this process and allow yourself to feel that toggle between stuck and clear, and then resolve it, you'll be more seasoned in knowing how to make the small adjustments and big leaps.

It takes tremendous courage to face painful truths— tremendous courage. Courage not only in admitting something challenging to yourself but courage in knowing that by taking in this truth, you'll be changed by it. And after it changes you and your inner landscape, it will demand change in your outside world, in the terrain of your lifestyle. Here, you find the profound pivot point of congruence. Here, doing what takes courage, bravery, and maybe a bit of holding-your-breath-and-jumping, is where you build a human life that is congruent with your Soul. Here, you do the work of integrating, no matter how hard, what your Soul has shown you and taught you.

Remember, your Soul and the divine forces within the Universe are kind, loving, forgiving. The Soul never demands a rush; it merely asks you to begin—and to take good care of yourself.

Often, a significant life change is made up of a series of small, step-by-step changes. Making life changes that reflect the truth of your Soul can be overwhelming, daunting, and scary, and it's okay—even advisable—to break these shifts down into more manageable pieces.

Remember the value of momentum, of that next right step. Remember, you have divine support in undertaking this process of transformation. Remember, the force of integrative action is forgiving, understanding, and patient. It'll wait for you, and then it'll nudge and remind you. This force will support and hold you, reminding you of your worth, value, and vision.

The integration phase of the healing journey will, ultimately, require you to audit your life, and no area will be overlooked or left to its own devices. The more you heal, the more thorough that process of life auditing becomes, and there's no other way, because the force of healing grows deeper and deeper at every pass. While this can be hard, the payoffs of living in congruence with your Soul outlast, outweigh, and outperform the alternative every single time.

Loss and Release on the Spiral Path of Awakening

There are times in the process of healing and awakening you'll know what you're working on is the right thing to work on, and the stuff you're releasing is what should be released, but you can't quite see the outcome. The finish line or the way your life looks *after* the process of transformation is obscured or unclear.

Within any process of awakening and transformation, there's always a space of *not quite yet*. These are spaces where the healing you've undergone and the integrative action you've taken, though right and powerful, have yet to give way to the next thing, to what's on the next horizon. This place can be hard, frustrating. After all, you've come so far, and you don't yet have the "reward" in hand.

For instance:

- You've released a relationship, and it's taken everything you had to do so. You sincerely want a new, right,
  loving, healthy relationship, but it hasn't materialized
  yet, and so you're feeling awfully lonely on the other
  side of this brave choice. You wonder if you're going
  to be alone forever or worry you're unlovable.

- You've sold your home, quit your job, gathered your
  belongings, and answered the Soul call to move across
  the country, but you don't feel connected to the com-
  munity or wired into that happiness of relocation yet.
  You wonder if you've made the right choice and feel
  very alone.

- You've left a longtime career to start a business, and
  several months in, you feel like the uphill climb is exhausting, and that optimistic energy of the start feels
  harder to harness. Costs are daunting, and being an
  entrepreneur is lonely in a way you didn't expect. You
  know you don't belong in your old job, but you're not
  sure you belong *here*, either.

- You've set boundaries with family members, and
  while you know this was right and healthy, their on-
  slaught of blame and scapegoating feels demoralizing.
  You're on the outs now, and while you don't necessar-

ily want back in, you haven't found a new place of comfort here on the outside.

So many of us experience this: the aloneness that comes when you heal, stop old patterns and habits, and become more conscious of your choices and relationships. The old familiar things that no longer feel right have gone away, but new, more fulfilling aspects of life haven't quite yet materialized. You know what was comfortable isn't right for you, but you miss it because, well, it was comfortable—and familiar. Some self-doubt might creep in, or fear may arise. *It feels like you're stuck between what you are no longer and what you have not quite yet become.*

When you've bravely created space in your life by releasing what no longer is congruent, but there is nothing to fill it yet, have faith, take heart, and trust your Soul.

This place tests you, for sure. When you've cleared away your old way of operating, powerfully breaking unhealthy patterns, you're always given a few opportunities to apply what you've learned—to test out your stamina. Here, conscious choice and self-care are paramount.

Tell yourself the truth about what your spirit needs to feel nourished and supported, and then choose those things—the people, relationships, daily practices, self-care routines, spiritual reminders, and healthy thoughts that create that reassuring stability.

Tend to your emotional and spiritual health, and allow yourself to feel and engage with your fear, grief, or sadness. Allowing these emotions to come up is part of this process of integration. When you're able to stay in this space and love yourself through it, you'll come to know yourself even more thoroughly.

Remember: when a seed is planted, it's growing tremendously below the surface. You don't see the development and growth of its elaborate root system, and you aren't able to fully comprehend the nourishment provided to that seed simply by virtue of being planted, lovingly, within the soil. You won't see it sprout immediately, but you know this, and you don't give up on it. You continue to water it and keep a tender eye out for the first signs of its emergence.

Treat yourself like this seed. Trust yourself and the forces of nature, of the Universe, and ground yourself in the faith that you have done something life-giving. Allow it time to grow.

Ultimately, your raised vibration will attract the new, more harmonious aspects of life you're longing for, but not before you're asked to affirm to yourself—to your

Soul—that the process of becoming more conscious, including the loss and release, is *all worth it.*

This part of the integration process is powerfully important and, ultimately, transformative. This place of not-quite-yet is where deep faith is fostered and cemented, where you come to trust yourself more than you ever have before, and where you lean on your intuition and remember your Soul.

Remember: the purpose of the steady pressure of life is to transform you and teach you about the profound intrinsic spiritual nature of who you are. Don't abandon yourself here—the Universe and its loyal forces certainly haven't. Stay right with the process and trust your Soul.

Everything in life transforms, and so will this.

SACRED INTENTION-SETTING:

Honoring Loss and Release on the Spiral Path

This intention offers you an opportunity to simply sit alongside any feelings of loss on your healing journey—without judgment or fear. Let's create a place for you to sit in the unknown and feel safe, supported, loved, and nourished.

When you're ready, read silently or aloud this intention:

As I sit alongside my Soul Fire, I welcome anything I am feeling or experiencing around the in-between or not-quite-yet stage of my healing journey. I allow my body and my spirit to feel any fear, anxiety, or loss that is necessary for me to experience. It is safe to feel what comes up, for as it does, I can honor it, allow it, and invite it to transform. What I feel here does not define me or call into question the sound decisions I have made thus far. Instead, what I experience here represents the parts of me needing more light, love, healing, and connection to my Soul. I allow this process to take place and remember that I am always divinely held and guided.

POWERING INTENTION
WITH ACTION

Consider how you might incorporate this vital seat of honoring into your life. We all need to pause and allow ourselves to feel what comes up at these momentous crossroads in life, and so, how might you give yourself that gift? Could you consider "stopping by" this place of nourishment once a week, by simply closing your eyes and envisioning? Would you like to appoint a physical object to remind you of this space and carry that object with you throughout your day? How might you remind yourself that it's perfectly normal and safe to move through periods of loss, uncertainty, fear, and unknown on your healing path?

Intentioned, Integrative
Rest on the Spiral Path

Rest is sacred. It's fundamentally necessary for us as humans—we literally cannot live without sleep and rest—and so it is the same for the Soul.

As you're journeying through your life and along this spiral path of self-actualization, you're going to arrive at times when you must rest. Your Soul will demand it. Your physical body and your human spirit will require it.

We can be inclined to skip this—to keep going to arrive at an outcome or get the hard part over with. Or, perhaps we've come to value the reflective action of healing, and we worry that stopping means we'll have broken down or lost our way. Certainly, our society values being busy over resting and so you might have some ingrained biases against allowing yourself to slow down or stop.

For some, resting can be one of the trickiest parts of the process.

When you feel the deep need to rest, don't ignore it. Consider this rest a sacred exercise and offer your Soul and your human body the kindness and care they need.

Are you familiar with the term lying fallow? It's a farming term describing a technique whereby a piece of farmland is left empty or unused for a season. The farmer allows that piece of land to become dormant so it can recover its fertility. Essentially, the ground, the soil, everything contained within it, are allowed to simply *be*.

Here, we find an inherent trust in nature and the value of, for a time, rest instead of action. This piece of land is left undisturbed and allowed to soak in the rain, absorb the sunlight, air in the moonlight, freeze in the cold, thaw in the warmth—taking in and releasing per the ebb and flow of natural forces. In lying fallow, this land is simply allowed to be within the larger, eternal, nourishing forces of nature, some of them seen and some of them unseen.

There is unequivocal value in allowing ourselves to lie fallow. In this practical and spiritual metaphor, nature encourages us to remember it is sometimes best to rest and recover—that doing so is necessary, sacred, and wise.

Sacred rest is life-restoring and life-giving. It is an act of both self-care and faith.

Our Souls prompt us to refine and grow and remind us that integrative rest is a welcome and restorative part of the process. Trust the seasonality of life: there is a time for nourishing, planting, harvesting, and yes, for lying fallow. Allow the wisdom of nature to validate your own internal wisdom. Sometimes, the next right action to take is to allow yourself sacred, integrative rest.

A Message from the Other Side

"As a human, you have made yourself busy and heavy with requirements. The truth is there is no requirement other than that of evolution. Everything begins and ends with evolution. Everything stems from and returns to evolution. Evolution does not rush, and it does not judge, it simply maintains its steady, intentioned pulse. Adopt the pace of nature to step in time with the pulse of evolution."

Gains and Gifts on the Spiral Path

Remember, as you journey, there is something much larger going on here. You are part of something divine and grand, and your awakening and evolution are of utmost importance to the Universe.

What feels immensely difficult or demands great change in your life will transform you if you let it. You are here to be changed, to become different, by what you learn, realize, encounter, and take in. You are here to remember, ultimately, that you are a Soul and that your path is a circular, loving one dedicated to you more consciously knowing who and what you are.

As you journey, remember and trust yourself, your Soul, and what you know:

- You Soul will not demand change that isn't in your *Highest and Best Honor.*

- You know, deep within your body and your being, what the next right step is.

- Looking at healing through the lens of self-love will never let you down; you can trust where it leads you and the pace it sets for you.

- Everything that's getting your attention—difficult emotions, frustrating relationships, stale jobs, continual patterns of conflict or difficulty, aches or pains or illness—is prompting you to go inward and to ask, sincerely and sacredly, *"What in me needs my attention? What in me is ready to become conscious so that I may work with it, heal it, and make healthier, more self-loving choices?"*

- If you look at your human life this way, you cannot stray far from your path. Everything in your human life is reflecting what you need to understand, know, look at, dive deeply into, heal, bring consciousness to, shift, gain awareness of, and change. Everything in your human life reflects what your Soul wants you to know and remember.

- You live in a Universe where the power of love and profound sacred guidance are always available.

- Your Soul knows why you incarnated and what themes and dynamics you came here to experience and heal. You can always, always, look to your Soul for guidance.

- Regarding your human existence as an ongoing, daily, spiritual experience and a never-ending conversation with higher, divine forces—including your Soul, your Spirit Guides, and your intuition—will never let you down.

 ## SACRED INTENTION-SETTING:
A Deep, Closing Breath

For this intention, return to your Soul Fire. Return to where we began. Return with all you now know and with any newly acquired insights, questions, curiosities, openness, clarity, or momentum. Return to your Soul Fire as a different, shifted you.

When you're ready, read silently or aloud this intention:

I return to my Soul Fire with new confidence, awareness, understanding, and self-compassion. I bring all I have learned and the parts of me that are shifted to my Soul Fire, opening in deep appreciation for myself. I love and appreciate myself and all I have done and continue to do to awaken, heal, evolve, and better know my Soul. I am powerful and devoted. I am gentle and fierce. I am a visioner who is guided. I have access, at all times, to this Soul Fire, this seat of perpetual healing. I am in charge of my choices and my path and am capable of becoming the most vibrant, whole, and alive version of myself in this lifetime. I offer myself love, gratitude, and admiration. I embrace my Soul with all that I am, and I know, deeply and truly, that I am loved.

**POWERING INTENTION
WITH ACTION**

Let's keep this one very simple. How might you take what you have learned and how you have shifted and do something with it that is profoundly and genuinely self-loving? How might you move forward from this place and love yourself more steadfastly and tenderly than ever?

You Can Do This

There are so many stories about lives interrupted or cut short, plans made and never fulfilled, hopes and dreams not realized, truth not told, and leaps not taken. These stories surround all of us, frequently touching us personally.

And we know: life can change, forever, in a moment.

Be present and brave. Take leaps. Stop letting fear hold you hostage. Don't give your power to family rules or societal pressures. When you find a piece of your life's truth, walk toward it, embrace it fiercely, and take it with you. Summon the courage to let go of what keeps you from stepping into those glorious pieces of truth.

Take responsibility and action; come into your power and deploy the forces of conscious choice and free will.

When you find something that makes you come alive, seize it—pull it with gusto into your life—and release whatever stands in its way.

You are and will be resolutely, steadfastly, and unconditionally supported in that endeavor by the Universe, your Soul, your loved ones on the Other Side, your Spirit Guides, and the loving divine forces that tenderly hold you.

You are here to make the most of this lifetime. You are here to do the very best you can with it, and to become the most vibrant, whole, authentic version of yourself.

Your success is already planned.

You can do this.

Acknowledgments

I am fortunate to have shared time and space throughout my life with people who have influenced and healed me, supported and loved me, and inspired and changed me. The last few years have been particularly transformative for me and it's impossible to not connect the creation of this book with this important era in my life. And so, I'd like to thank some people who, very specifically, have made magnificent contributions during this time of awakening, healing, and evolution.

To Anna Bannister, my brilliant card-flipper, emotional safe place, ah-ha-moment purveyor, soulmate from the depths: What you have done for me, for an awfully long time, but particularly since the very magical April of 2018, has been a display of dedication, loyalty, vulnerability, intimacy, kindness, generosity, and love like I have never seen or known. I, very literally, could not have arrived here, at this version of me, without you.

To Jeanine Tousignant, my Soul sister, past life journey-er, fearless traveler, lunchtime process partner, curb-crying sentry: What you have done for me and given to me can never be fully repaid. You have taught me how to receive, and how to feel worthy of true giving. You are the epito-me of loving generosity. Your gifts, in all their forms, have made me feel ready, safe, willing, supported, and loved. I am profoundly and deeply grateful to and for you.

To Mike Degnan: From colleague to friend to family, how lucky I am to have you in my life. Thank you for standing next to me and with me. You have redefined so much in my life with your steadfast, kind, gentle, uncondi-tional support and love. You are one of the very best men I have ever known. You have changed the course of my life because of that, and I am more whole because of you.

To my grandmother, Betty Benway: I feel you and miss you every single day. Thank you for visiting me so often. I love you. So much.

To Joe Profetto, Scott Wolfram, and Sappho Wolfram: For your wise, Soul-filled guidance and love. Each of you has changed my life for the better. Thank you for accom-panying and supporting me on my Soul journey.

To Johanna Hattendorf and Lisa Stedman: For all the real-ness, roaring laughter, torrents of tears, hairy eyeballs and eyerolls, psychic fun and not-so-fun, energetic jour-neys across the dimensions, crystals, rocks, and knowing who needed what and when. Thank you for illustrating true love, steadfast partnership, safe intimacy, and interpersonal honesty. I am changed because of each of you. I am changed because of what you are together.

There are people who drew this book out of me, lovingly escorting me out of my own way, so what was meant to be could be:

Brady Sadler, thank you for being one of these people, not only when it came to this book, but to my life's journey. You have been a soulmate from the get-go and I am honored that our friendship has stood the test of time. I'm with you all the way and beyond, my friend.

Heather Doyle Fraser, you brought me the gift of a lifetime: the opportunity and invitation to love myself more wholly, fiercely, and unconditionally than ever before. This book—my rebirth—wouldn't exist without you. Thank you.

Janice Gregory, thank you for seeing me—truly seeing me—all this time. You saw me before I saw myself; and now, you see me when I'm afraid, daunted, or unsure. People like you don't come along every day. I trust you, I love you, and I'm deeply grateful for you.

Jacquelyn Fletcher, thank you for sacredly commanding me to create this book. Your invitation was the catalyst for something life-changing and divine. I am forever grateful to you.

Paul Boynton, thank you for our talks, our candor, and our friendship. Thank you for your guidance and gracious generosity in this process.

To colleagues, friends, and chosen family who have walked, selflessly and lovingly, with me on my journey:

Ellen McCahon, you are one fantastic human being. You set the most endearing, graceful, generous bar for what it means to live in love and truth. I am deeply inspired by you.

Jay Martin, for your surprise and thrilling appearance in my life. I'm so glad you're here. Life is better with you in it.

Jeff Kipperman, thank you for your brilliance, compassion, and generosity. Your presence in my life has been transformative.

Jennifer Baldi, for your friendship, beautiful humor, brilliant artistry, and steadfast support. You mean so much to me and I am so grateful to have you with me on this journey. I admire you greatly and love you deeply.

Jessica Gelvin, for showing up, being brave, and doing it all with gorgeous honesty. You are loving, real, and honest. Thank you for being my Soul sister.

Julie Carter, for your fierce advocacy, patient teaching, delightful friendship, and fiery loyalty. I count myself lucky to have you in my life. Thank you.

Laura Monica, for your honesty, generosity, and kindness. You and I know what you have done. Yours is the fiercest kind of love. Thank you.

Linda Monica and Dick Horan, for your kindness, love, and profound generosity. Your mark has been indelibly made—on me and my family—and I will forever be grateful.

MB Lufkin, for your tried-and-true friendship. Thank you for your unwavering support, from day one, and for the depths we share.

About the Author

Katie Benway is a psychic, medium, certified life coach, speaker, and writer. She is a natural psychic and medium, experiencing these intuitive connections beginning in very early childhood. Today, Katie uses her psychic and mediumship abilities, along with her professional training and innate skill as a life coach, to offer insight, clarity, guidance, accompaniment, and healing to clients through individual sessions, coaching, and workshops.

She values engaging in deep, meaningful, truth-centered healing work and creating a safe, supported space in which individuals are able to connect with their higher selves, inner awareness, and personal power.

Katie helps her clients clear old karmic and past life patterns; identify and heal disempowering beliefs, patterns, and conditioning; and connect with loved ones on the Other Side and divine guides. Katie believes that the work of helping people heal, raise their consciousness, and become the seat of their own power is why she has the innate psychic and spiritual connections she does.

Katie created Intrepid Eleven, LLC, in 2010, offering in-person and distance readings, personal coaching, and healing sessions. Since then, Katie has provided thousands of readings and healing sessions to people from across the United States, Canada, Europe, and Australia. Many of Katie's clients call her their "psychic life coach."

Meanwhile, as a speaker and teacher, Katie has presented to a variety of groups, large and small, in-person and online, in intimate workshops and at large conferences, on topics including intuition, conscious parenting, past lives, healing subconsciously held belief systems, and personal spiritual empowerment.

Prior to creating Intrepid Eleven, Katie spent 12 years in business as a marketing and communications professional. She is based in Concord, New Hampshire, and has two young sons. You can find Katie online at www.IntrepidEleven.com and on Instagram, Facebook, and Twitter at the Intrepid Eleven handle.